Fearless Female
SOLDIERS, EXPLORERS, AND AVIATORS

Agatha Christie

TRAVELER, ARCHAEOLOGIST, AND AUTHOR

MEGHAN M. ENGSBERG CUNNINGHAM

Cavendish Square
New York

Published in 2018 by Cavendish Square Publishing, LLC
243 5th Avenue, Suite 136, New York, NY 10016

First Edition

Library of Congress Cataloging-in-Publication Data

Names: Cunningham, Meghan Engsberg.
Title: Agatha Christie: traveler, archaeologist, and
author / Meghan Engsberg Cunningham.
Description: New York : Cavendish Square, 2018. |
Series: Fearless female soldiers, explorers, and aviators | Includes index.
Identifiers: ISBN 9781502627551 (library bound) | ISBN 9781502627568 (ebook)
Subjects: LCSH: Christie, Agatha, 1890-1976–Juvenile literature. |
Authors, English–20th century–Biography–Juvenile literature. |
Detective and mystery stories–Authorship–Juvenile literature.
Classification: LCC PR6005.H66 C85 2018 | DDC 823′.912–dc23

Editorial Director: David McNamara
Editor: Stacy Orlando
Copy Editor: Nathan Heidelberger
Associate Art Director: Amy Greenan
Designer: Stephanie Flecha
Production Coordinator: Karol Szymczuk
Photo Research: J8 Media

The photographs in this book are used by permission and through the courtesy of: Cover Popperfoto/Getty Images; p. 4 Mondadori Portfolio/Getty Images; p. 10 AGE fotostock/Alamy Stock Photo; p. 12 Wikimedia Commons/File:Archibald Christie 1915.jpg/Public Domain; p. 17 Pictorial Press Ltd/Alamy Stock Photo; p. 21 Derek Harper/Wikimedia Commons/File:Plaque, Barton Road - geograph.org.uk - 674119.jpg/CC BY SA 2.0; p. 22 The Print Collector/Print Collector/Getty Images; p. 26, 37 The Everett Collection Historical/Alamy Stock Photo; p. 29 CSU Archives/ The Everett Collection; p. 30 Emma Childs; p. 39 Sueddeutsche Zeitung Photo/ Alamy Stock Photo; p. 42 Annie Eagle/Alamy Stock Photo; p. 46 Pierre Petit/ Wikimedia Commons/File:Richard Wagner, Paris, 1861.jpg/Public Domain; p. 48 The Everett Collection; p. 53 Angus McComiskey/Getty Images; p. 57 Hulton Archive/Getty Images; p. 59 H. F. Davis/Topical Press Agency/Getty Images; p. 61 Planet News Archive/SSPL/Getty Images; p. 68 Three Lions/Hulton Archive/ Getty Images; p. 70, 91, 94 Popperfoto/Getty Images; p. 75, 87 Julie Alissi/J8 Media; p. 81 Bentley Archive/Popperfoto/Getty Images; p. 88 Chronicle/Alamy Stock Photo; p. 102 Movie Poster Image Art/Getty Images; p. 105 Dave Hogan/ Getty Images; p. 109 Luis Veiga/Getty Images; p. 113 Express/Getty Images.

Printed in the United States of America

Contents

1 World Wars, English Society, and Detective Fiction 5

2 Childhood Dreams 27

3 Christie Embraces Adulthood 49

4 The Great Detective Novel 71

5 The Agatha Christie Phenomenon 95

Glossary 114

Chronology. 116

Further Information. 119

Bibliography 121

Index 124

About the Author 128

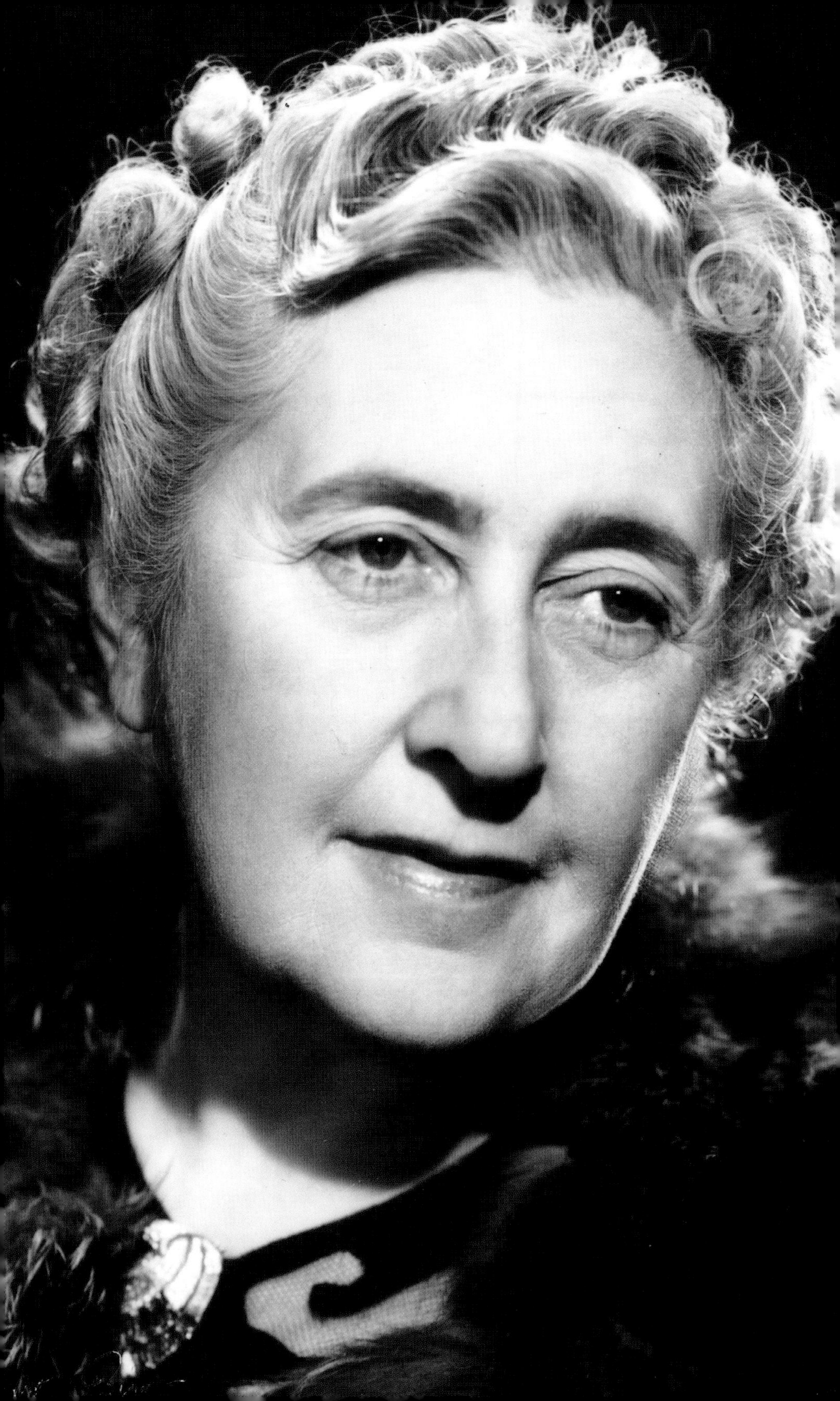

one

World Wars, English Society, and Detective Fiction

"Some prolific writers have made a deep impression on the public consciousness. Consider Agatha Christie, arguably the most popular writer of the twentieth century."
—Stephen King

Dame Agatha Mary Clarissa Christie, Lady Mallowan, DBE, was one of the most prolific writers of detective fiction in the world. During her life, she wrote 72 novels, 160 short stories, and 15 stage plays, one of which, *The Mousetrap*, is the world's longest-running play. Many of her

Opposite: Agatha Christie, famous British mystery writer

novels have been adapted for film and television, and some texts have even been adapted multiple times. While Christie is most famous for her creative writing, she also lived a unique, fascinating life. She spent a good portion of time working at archaeological dig sites in the Middle East and traveling the world, and her experiences not only enriched her life but also made the great quantity of her published written works even more fascinating.

For a woman born in England in 1890, making a living as a writer or an archaeologist might have seemed unusual. Christie grew up in an upper-middle-class family that, like many other economically similar families of the time, struggled to maintain their wealth. She was expected to grow up and have a life just like many women at that time: to become a respectable lady, marry well, and be a good wife and mother. Although Christies's family did not anticipate that she would have a career and be a trailblazing author, they did encourage her to be creative and use her imagination. This indulgence led Christie to idealize both her childhood experiences and her mother. As an adult, Christie constantly prioritized her mother above all other relationships, even over her husbands. Later in life, Christie struggled to recreate the sense of security and happiness she experienced as a child.

Her somewhat idyllic environment combined with the turbulent world she grew up in certainly influenced Christie's body of work. Her writing career began in earnest in 1920 with the publication of her novel *The Mysterious Affair at Styles*, which she wrote during World War I. During this time, the growing middle class developed an appetite for detective fiction. This demand, along with Christie's talent for writing, helped to fashion her success.

After the war, Christie began traveling extensively, and she spent the majority of her life traveling to and assisting on archaeological digs. Agatha Christie has been praised as a feminist, a trailblazer, and an adventurer. While all of these adjectives can be applied to her today, she would likely have dismissed them all and stated that she simply was a writer. Regardless, Christie thrived when she was traveling to new exotic locations and writing.

Life in Torquay, England

When Christie was born in 1890, Great Britain, or the United Kingdom, was the richest nation in the world and had the world's highest standard of living. Also known as the British Empire, it consisted of England, Australia, Canada, and many other countries around the world. The British Empire was as big and powerful as it would ever be. England, the primary country in the United Kingdom, was one of the first countries to **industrialize**, and it had a large number of working-class people. In addition, the standard of living was much higher in Britain than any other country.

The standard of living was so much higher than the rest of Europe, and it was common for the affluent British to travel abroad often, especially to France. In fact, if a family suffered financial difficulties, they would often choose to rent out their English home for a while and live in another country for a year or two. The difference in the cost of living between the countries would allow the family to pay off their debts. Christie's family lived for a while in France when she was a young girl to save some money.

The Miller Family

Agatha Christie was born on September 15, 1890. She was the third child of Frederick Alvah Miller and Clarissa (Clara) Miller. Her sister, Margaret Frary (Madge), and her brother, Louis Montant (Monty), were eleven and ten years old, respectively, at the time of Christie's birth. The Miller family was considered upper middle class, as were the majority of the families and residents in the town of Torquay, where the family lived.

Frederick Miller was an American educated in Switzerland and living abroad when he met Clara Margaret Boehmer, and they were married in 1878. After the wedding, the Millers lived off of Frederick's investments and properties in New York. Frederick intended for the two to return to New York to manage his properties, but they instead stayed in England. When Frederick was away traveling, Clara purchased a home in Torquay, England, on a whim. The two chose to live permanently in Torquay instead, and after deciding to stay, Frederick never actively worked again.

Frederick lived as if he had a limitless income. His daily life consisted of elaborate meals, outings to the Royal Torquay Yacht Club, and shopping. While his habit of spending and never worrying about money helped Christie live in a dreamlike childhood, it made life after his death extremely difficult for the family because of the state of their finances. Christie would spend much of her adult life struggling to live comfortably with her upper-middle-class background and her middle-class work ethic. In periods of financial challenges, however, Christie would follow in her father's footsteps and spend money as if it would always be there.

Christie did not spend her childhood in the company of siblings and children her own age, but instead with her parents and the many Miller servants. Her older siblings, Madge and Monty, attended boarding schools and were away from home for much of Christie's childhood. Instead of playing with other children, Christie's days revolved around her mother. Clara remained the center of Christie's world, even into adulthood. Many biographers have noted that Clara, rather than either of Christie's husbands, was the great love of Christie's life. In this way, perhaps Christie's childhood planted the seeds that allowed her to grow into a trailblazing and courageous woman.

Society's Expectations

Since Christie was such a prolific writer, it might be easy to assume that she had attended school and excelled in writing. Instead, Christie learned at home, with various lessons given by her mother or father. Once Christie was older, it would have been normal for her to follow her siblings to a boarding school, but she only attended briefly after her father's death. In fact, it was not out of the ordinary for a girl of Christie's economic level to stay at home rather than be sent to formal schooling full time at the turn of the twentieth century. The Millers did provide Christie with a **governess** for a brief time in France, but she never had a full-time teacher at home, unlike most upper-middle-class children in the early 1900s. Instead, it seems Clara did her best to fill the role of a governess.

After reaching a certain age, it was expected that a young woman of the upper classes be announced to society. This was most often done at a special event known as a coming-out party or a debut. The party fulfilled multiple social purposes

Agatha and her mother, Clara, demonstrate their close bond in this portrait.

and was sometimes even held before the royal court of the United Kingdom. The main reason for the party was to allow parents the opportunity to display their daughter to eligible bachelors so she could eventually marry. The gathering also provided single men the occasion to socialize with other single women and find wives.

With this cultural ritual, Christie met the expectations of society. However, Christie came out in Cairo, Egypt, and it was not until a few years later that she did get married. For much of her adult life, it seemed that all Christie wanted was to be a successful wife and build companionship with her husband. In many ways, Christie took the steps that an average well-off woman would take as she grew up and entered adulthood in early twentieth-century England. She learned to read and write at home, came out to society, and got married. Women at that time were not expected to have a career or be independent, as a woman born today might be.

Marriage

As a child and young adult, Christie identified marriage as her fate, part of her female destiny. This attitude was completely normal for the world in which she lived. Aspiring to marriage was part of her upbringing, and she never questioned it. Most upper-middle-class English girls did not seek out careers. Their learning was instead focused on becoming desirable candidates for marriage. Christie was not an exception, and in this way she differed from her contemporary Dorothy L. Sayers, another crime fiction writer, who disdained the marriage tradition.

Biographers of Agatha Christie have speculated that she never felt trapped by marriage or the institution because she always felt free through her imagination and writing. She lived within her own brain, imagining and creating things. Christie loved being a woman and doing traditional female things. She had grown up surrounded by women, but in adulthood she somehow adapted to being in a "man's" world as well. Christie was not hampered by the expectations of society.

Archibald Christie, pictured here in 1915, was promoted until he became a colonel in the Royal Flying Corps.

Instead, she absorbed the culture around her, and so much of it would pervade her writing throughout her career.

The World Wars

When World War I began, Agatha was in a relationship with Archibald Christie, the man who would become her husband. Agatha and Archie met in 1912, and their relationship was often tumultuous. Archie was an army officer, and the start of the war motivated the two to marry because he was to be stationed in Farnborough in northeast England, about 160 miles (260 kilometers) away from Torquay. After a quarrel, Archie proposed a quick wedding, and on Christmas Eve 1914, the two married. Shortly after the wedding, Agatha and Archie returned to their separate lives. Without World War I,

Agatha might have never done more than the little writing she accomplished before her marriage. It could be said that the time apart from her husband encouraged her to pursue a career and life as an independent woman.

World War I

World War I, also known as the First World War and the Great War, marked the end of Christies's young adulthood. The conflict began in the summer of 1914 as a **diplomatic** crisis in Europe, specifically in Austria-Hungry, when Archduke Franz Ferdinand was assassinated by a Yugoslav nationalist. On July 28, 1914, Austria-Hungry declared war on Serbia. From that initial declaration of war, countries began taking sides. Russia supported Serbia, and Germany invaded Belgium, Luxemburg, and then France. At that time, the United Kingdom declared war on Germany. By the fall of that year, the group of Central powers included Germany, Austria-Hungary, and the Ottoman Empire (including what is today known as Turkey). They were aligned against the Allies of Great Britain, France, Russia, Italy, and Japan, with the United States joining later in 1917.

The Allies eventually defeated the Central powers. When the Treaty of Versailles was negotiated in 1919, many thought the terms would not allow another war to happen. Signed on June 28, 1919, the treaty burdened Germany. As a result of the treaty and other turmoil within Germany, peace only lasted for twenty years before the Second World War would begin. World War I did lead to the downfall of four empires: Germany, Austria-Hungry, Russia, and Turkey. It did not, however, end all wars. Many of the problems involved in World War I reignited and led to World War II.

One of the greatest tolls of World War I was the human cost. More than nine million soldiers died, and twenty-one million more were wounded throughout the duration of the conflict. In addition, millions of other people fell victim to the influenza epidemic that the war helped spread. Civilian casualties also numbered nearly ten million. World War I was fought with trench warfare, which was the use of ditches in which troops were somewhat protected from enemy fire. The weaponry and close proximity of the soldiers made the war especially gruesome. World War I was also the first war to be fought in the air, with air forces and fighter pilots.

The United Kingdom, London, and the Great War

The United Kingdom initially entered the war when Germany invaded neutral Belgium, whom they were allied with. On August 4, 1914, Great Britain declared war on Germany. As part of the conflict, Germany carried out over one hundred bombing raids on Great Britain, causing much destruction in both the countryside and in London. Airplanes and bombs were used for the first time, and London was often a target.

In addition, the economy of England and the United Kingdom changed. Prior to the war, much of England's wealth came from international trade. The war disrupted the trade and was never recovered. While Americans remember the years after World War I as a period of economic prosperity known as the Roaring Twenties, England was growing poorer and unemployment was rising. The upper and middle classes of England feared the working classes. In 1918 and 1926, there were massive general strikes, during which work across all industries came to a halt. The conditions in England worsened in the 1930s as the Great Depression in America spread to

Europe. Christie would draw on these tensions in some of her early novels, especially the Tommy and Tuppence mysteries.

The beginning of the Great War was shocking to Christie and her mother. Neither of them was very attuned to politics, and there had not been a major European war for nearly a generation. When England became involved, the Royal Flying Corps was one of the first forces to be mobilized, and this included Archie, who quickly saw action in France. One of his last letters to Christie before he received orders summarizes the challenges she would have during the war: "You will be very brave won't you Angel; it will be very hard to sit at home and do nothing, and I am afraid you will have money troubles too." Christie was incapable of doing nothing, and both World War I and World War II would be the two most industrious periods of her life.

Christie and the Great War

The need for health care and health professionals was extremely high during the war. This provided Christie an opportunity to volunteer and work independently. She joined the Voluntary Aid Detachment, or VAD. She worked at a hospital in her hometown of Torquay as an unpaid VAD nurse. Because she was beside herself with worry and anxiety when Archie was on the front lines, she appreciated her opportunity to work at the VAD. Torquay was one of the locations where the British brought boats of their wounded, so the need for health care was very great.

Prior to the war, Christie had taken classes on bandaging and first aid as a way to occupy time. Early on at the hospital, she cleaned and scrubbed and did unglamorous odd jobs. Once she gained more knowledge, she was able to tend to wounded soldiers. She was also responsible for assisting the doctors, and she helped maintain morale among both doctors and patients. Christie worked extremely hard; between October 1914 and December 1916 she provided 3,400 hours of unpaid work for the VAD.

The war effort exemplified Christie's work ethic and also provided her the background medical knowledge she would need to write about poisons in her future detective and mystery fiction. After recovering from a bout of influenza along with bronchitis, Christie returned to her work at the hospital and found that an **apothecary** shop had opened with two women in charge, a local doctor's wife, Mrs. Ellis, and another woman by the name of Eileen Morris. The dispensary provided a unique opportunity. Christie joined Mrs. Ellis and Miss Morris as an assistant and began to study for examinations that would qualify her to dispense medicine.

In 1917, Christie qualified as an apothecaries' assistant, or dispenser. To qualify as a dispenser, Christie learned the practical dispensing from Mrs. Ellis, and Eileen Morris taught her the physics and chemistry. She struggled at first but grew to like the subjects because she had a talent for mathematics, especially algebra.

Working at the dispensary provided Christie better hours than her standard work at the VAD. She worked alternate mornings and afternoons and was able to do a good amount of housework and cooking. Even though she was a newlywed, she still wanted to help keep the Miller family home running, and needed to make money for her own family unit with Archie. According to Red Cross accounting, Christie worked 3,400 unpaid hours from October 1914 through December 1916. From 1917 through the end of her service in September

Posters like this one advertised the need for nurses, as well as other occupations, in the VAD to support the war effort.

1918, she was paid an annual rate of £17 (equal to about $1,270 in 2017) for her work at the dispensary.

Because of the war, Christie spent her life as a newlywed separated from her husband. The two were able to spend his leave together in October 1915 but were separated for their first anniversary and Christmas. In 1917, Archie had three periods of leave, but the time the two spent together was more like a vacation than a marriage. Eventually, Archie was stationed back in England in September 1918 as a colonel in the Air Ministry.

When Archie returned to Great Britain with the rank of colonel, Christie left the hospital and her position as a dispenser. They searched for a furnished flat to share and start their lives together, even though they had been married for nearly four years. Archie was twenty-nine years old, and Agatha was twenty-eight. Both had seen much suffering, pain, grief, and death over the course of the war—which didn't officially end until November 11, 1918, Armistice Day.

The war provided Christie with a way to earn a living and a body of knowledge that she carried into her work as a writer. In fact, in the middle of the war, she tried writing her first piece of detective fiction, partially inspired by her time in the dispensary.

World War II

World War II, or the Second World War, in many ways revisited the unfinished issues of World War I. World War II lasted from 1939 to 1945 and involved nearly every country in the world. The countries formed two military alliances: the Axis and the Allies. The Axis powers consisted of Germany, Italy, and Japan, and the Allied Powers primarily of France, Great Britain, the United States, the Soviet Union, and China.

World War II began in 1939 when the German dictator, Adolf Hitler, ordered the invasion of Poland on August 31, 1939. Three days later, on September 3, Great Britain and France declared war on Germany in support of Poland.

By the time World War II happened, Christie was happily married to her second husband, Sir Max Mallowan, a prominent British archaeologist. She was also an established, successful author. As could be expected, the war changed their daily lives. Owing to the growing unrest, the couple had to leave a dig site in Iraq, where the routine of their lives had taken shape. Christie was resilient. She had survived World War I, and she accepted the start of another war as inevitable. After hearing the statement of war from the prime minister, Christie remained steadfast. She knew the war would be a struggle, but domestic tasks would need to be done just the same. They would continue to be her responsibility, and she would contribute to the war effort as best she could.

World War II drastically changed the United Kingdom. The colonial holdings throughout the world became independent. When India was officially decolonized in 1947, the British Empire was essentially over. Many of the former territories formed what is now know as the Commonwealth of Nations along with Great Britain. Yet England was no longer the richest country in the world. It was just one among other struggling European nations. The wartime rationing of food and clothes would continue into the 1950s. The loss of wealth and power was hard for many British people to come to terms with. Many of Christie's detective stories, especially those written in the 1950s and 1960s, dealt indirectly with the change in power and prestige.

Torquay, Devon

Christie was born in and grew up in Torquay, Devon, in Southwest England. Torquay was a town originally built on agriculture and fishing as the major industries. By 1890, it was becoming a fashionable seaside resort town. Early in the nineteenth century, the town was frequented by members of the Royal Navy. Torquay became renowned for its healthful climate. It even had a brush with fame when Napoleon III recuperated there. Today, Torquay is still a seaside resort town, although it appeals to tourists much more than it did when the Miller family resided there.

The home that the Miller family owned in Torquay was given the name Ashfield. Ashfield was a large, comfortable villa with a sprawling lawn and small woods outside. It had three stories, several chimneys, and a conservatory. Although large and comfortable, the home was not ostentatious. As a child, Christie especially enjoyed playing outside in the woods.

Christie loved Ashfield. She helped her mother maintain the home until her mother's death, and she was loath to sell the home until she was nearly fifty years old. In fact, when Ashfield was demolished in the 1960s, twenty years after Christie had sold it, she cried. Today a plaque commemorates the site where it stood. Christie would spend much of her adult life trying to find another property to replace Ashfield.

The site where Christie's childhood home once stood is commemorated with this plaque.

The Popularity of Detective Fiction

Crime and detective fiction had begun to grow in popularity during World War I. Readers wanted to escape from the turmoil around them. The attractiveness of detective stories was also great again during World War II (1939–1945), similarly for the escapism they provided readers but also for the formulaic, ordered world they presented. At the end of each novel, the mystery was solved and everything revealed.

Christie's writing of detective fiction came at a perfect time, culturally. Edgar Allan Poe, an American writer who lived from

"HOLMES GAVE ME A SKETCH OF THE EVENTS."

Sherlock Holmes and Dr. John Watson are depicted discussing a case in this illustration by Sidney E. Paget.

1809 to 1849, invented the detective story, although he only wrote four such stories. The first author to fully explore detective fiction was Arthur Conan Doyle, the creator of Sherlock Holmes. Doyle's Sherlock Holmes series appeared from 1887 to 1927, and some of Doyle's writings overlapped with Christie's. Sherlock Holmes captured the reading public's imagination, and they were ready for more.

By the time Christie was writing, a few conventions of the **genre** had been established. In the stories, there needed to be one detective, and in many of the popular novels, the protagonist also tended to be eccentric. Sherlock Holmes was definitely peculiar, and Christie's Poirot and Miss Marple also fit in this category. Another convention was that the detective must solve the mystery through deduction and scientific methods with a lack of emotion.

The Growing Middle-Class Audience

When Christie was a child, the Miller family was neither independently wealthy nor in the working class. They were part of the growing middle class. Christie's basic needs were never in question, but the Millers struggled. Since neither of her parents was actively engaged in a steady profession, it was difficult to keep up with household expenses, maintain properties, and pay servants.

As Christie aged and began growing her writing career, the middle class also grew. In England, especially in London, during the 1930s, incomes were rising for those who held jobs—although jobs were harder and harder to find. More people were buying cars and owning their homes. Many were still dealing with the trauma of World War I or the increasing turmoil of the impending World War II, but detective fiction

Women's Suffrage

Today it is hard to believe that women were not always able to vote. When Christie was born in 1890, the women's suffrage movement in the United Kingdom was gaining popularity, but women like her mother and grandmother had never been able to vote. British women began clamoring for the right to vote in 1835, when a law passed that explicitly stated women could not vote. The campaign gained momentum, although it was put on the back burner during World War I because all resources were focused on the war effort.

In 1918, wealthy, propertied women were given the ability to vote. The Representation of the People Act of 1918 enfranchised women over the age of thirty who met minimum property qualifications. It would be ten more years until all women were able to vote. In 1928, the Representation of the People (Equal Franchise) Act gave all women over the age of twenty-one the right to vote.

Agatha Christie was born nearly forty years before women had the right to vote in the United Kingdom. By the time she gained the right to vote, Christie was writing and supporting herself financially, and she was in the process of divorcing her husband. She lived an exceptionally apolitical life, especially in her early adulthood. She was not a part of the women's suffrage movement, and she had little concern about the birth of the Labour Party or the actions of David Lloyd George, the prime minister, all of which were taking place at the same time.

was not overly intellectual and appealed to a wide range of readers, including the middle class. While Christie would often hold aristocratic values, she depended on both her and her husband actively working.

Agatha Christie became a famous author who lived a unique life traveling and working as an archaeologist. She was able to write prolifically, more than any other woman, while working within the confines of early twentieth-century England. Although Christie was raised in a different manner than some upper-middle-class English children, her trailblazing career was not necessarily a product of her upbringing but rather of the changing British society Christie was a part of from childhood through World War II.

Although Christie became a successful, self-funding and self-sufficient author, she always longed for the idyllic days of her childhood. Her especially close relationship with her mother, Clara, and her notions of relationships and marriage often made Christie seem childlike up until she was well into her sixties.

two

Childhood Dreams

"One of the luckiest things that can happen to you in life is, I think, to have a happy childhood." —Agatha Christie

When Agatha Mary Clarissa Miller was born in 1890, her parents were much older than the average parents with a newborn baby in the nineteenth century. Clara was thirty-six years old, which was seen as extremely old for having children, and was younger than Frederick, who was in his forties. Christie's older siblings, Madge and Monty, were already eleven and ten years old, and Madge was already living away from home and attending boarding school when Christie was born. The difference in age between Christie and her siblings, as well as the age of her parents,

Oppostite: Christie, seen here at about ten years of age, was an imaginative child.

would influence how Christie would receive an education and socialize with her peers.

Christie's Home: Ashfield

Christie lived an extremely contented and safe childhood at Ashfield in Torquay—a home she absolutely adored. She spent much of her time playing with her animals and imaginary friends. If one was looking for hints that Christie was to be a prolific writer of fiction, her imagination as a child might have been one of those hints. Christie was fond of playing imaginary games. One of her favorite pastimes was to imagine funerals, and she would often place flowers on the grave of her beloved canary, Kiki. While Christie loved to use her imagination, she used it primarily for happy and safe scenarios. She liked to please people and be good, moral, and virtuous. As a child, she did not have any interest in poisons or murders that would have hinted toward her future writing detective fiction.

Besides her pets, and her imaginary friends and creatures, Christie spent time with her parents, the family servants, and the few people she was extremely familiar with. To those outside of Ashfield, Christie often seemed shy and **reticent**. Even as an adult, Christie had trouble summoning the courage to walk into a shop or converse with someone while she was running an errand.

Christie always described her childhood as extremely happy, despite the monetary struggles her family would face. When Christie was five years old, Frederick learned that there was no more money in his estate. He tried to find a job but had very little luck. He died when Christie was eleven and left the family in even more financial distress. In fact, his death

Agatha Christie, age eight, and her father, Frederick, spend time together outside.

and poor health were likely hastened by the constant money troubles and worry. Despite the financial concerns, the Millers managed to cobble together an upper-middle-class life. Christie's happiness was intact, even when rumors circulated that they often ate simple meals of rice pudding.

Servants at Ashfield

Early in her life, Christie recognized that the servants employed at Ashfield were crucial to maintaining the household and her own comfort. Clara taught her that servants are highly trained professionals. They were respected, skilled individuals, crucial to maintaining the household, and not simply companions for Christie and servers for the Millers. Both Nursie, Christie's nanny, and Jane, the cook, were extremely important people to Christie. When reflecting on her childhood in her autobiography, Christie wrote that if she were a child during modern times (the 1960s and 1970s), she would miss servants. To her, a good servant was a worthy person with real social standing. Later in life and short of money, Christie considered becoming a parlor maid to help support her and Archie.

A watercolor rendering of Ashfield by artist Emma Childs shows off the sunroom of Christie's beloved home.

As a child, Christie liked safety and order, and she enjoyed the calm yet busy atmosphere of the kitchen. She was also interested in the practical domestic tasks of a home: the way the pastry was made, ironing done, or dresses starched. Christie took much interest in servants and how they ran a household, and she even featured them prominently as characters in many of her works when she began writing mysteries.

Young Christie was already fascinated with the simple and ordinary. She also liked to observe and figure out how things worked; this included people and complex relationships. She seemed particularly interested in the balance of power between people, and how they used, or did not use, that influence. Christie enjoyed watching her parents provide instructions to the servants, but she also saw the strength and expertise when the cook or other servants were preparing for meals and events. The ability to pay attention to these details would be the foundation for so many of her detective novels.

Although it would have made more financial sense for Ashfield to be sold in 1901 upon Frederick's death, Christie—only eleven years old—insisted the property be saved, and her mother acquiesced. Because they had to keep Ashfield on a limited budget, maintenance fell behind, and they could only retain two young and inexpensive maids. For a while, Jane, the cook, refused to leave. Jane, however, had a hard time adjusting from cooking lobsters and elaborate creations for the family to simple meals of macaroni and cheese for just Clara and Christie alone. Eventually Jane also left Ashfield for a new opportunity.

The Matriarchy at Ashfield

Even though she had a close companionship with her father, Christie was part of a strong **matriarchy**. The women, from Christie's grandparents down to servants like Jane and Nursie, were much stronger than the men in the family, Frederick and Christie's brother, Monty. Christie's full name, Agatha Mary Clarissa Miller, honored her mother, grandmother, and one of her mother's favorite novels, titled *Agatha's Husband*. As a child, Clara also lived with her aunt, Margaret Miller, and it was through her that she met Frederick, who was Margaret's stepson. Christie knew her step-grandmother as "Auntie-Grannie." Clara's mother, Mary Ann, was known as "Grannie B." Young Christie knew both women well, and she spent quite a bit of time at both of their homes. Clara also told countless stories featuring both women that captivated Christie's imagination.

Because of the tutelage of her mother, among others, Christie always knew that women were a source of strength. Clara would tell lots of stories about her ancestors and relations. Despite Christie's own future as a dispenser, writer, and archaeologist, she would never consider herself a feminist. Even toward the end of her life and the height of her success, she believed that women were at their best and strongest when involved in household and domestic tasks. The strong matriarchy that supported her taught Christie to value marriage, but it also gave her the self-reliance to forge her own way—which helped her take on a career as a writer.

When Frederick passed away, the bond between Christie and her mother became unbreakable, almost unusual. Despite having two other children, Clara lived for her youngest child alone, and Christie reciprocated. For a long time after

Frederick Miller's passing, Clara was beside herself with grief. Christie missed her father but was satisfied with her mother's companionship. Clara's sorrow was overpowering, and at one point she became extremely ill. Even though she was only eleven years old, Christie worried about her mother and did her best to take care of her. Christie would stand outside Clara's bedroom at night for hours on end to ensure that her mother was still breathing. The grief both of them felt brought them closer together.

The World Away from Ashfield

Although Christie truly treasured her home and childhood at Ashfield, she had some fantastic travel experiences as a child. In 1896, when Christie was six, Frederick was working to combat the financial struggles he was facing. He decided to rent out Ashfield to acquire more income, and the family moved to France for a year. While this might seem like a more expensive endeavor today, as discussed earlier, for the upper class, or **gentry**, this was a common practice at the turn of the twentieth century. The difference in the cost of living between England and France helped the Millers stay financially sound for a time.

Going to France with her family was Christie's first travel experience. Although she was away from Ashfield for the first time, Christie did not miss her home as they visited Pau, Cauterets, Paris, and Brittany. Seeing the Pyrenees, a mountain range in France, was a new experience for her. She had longed to see mountains, but the trip was quite different than the young Christie had imagined. Even with that disenchantment, Christie would spend her whole life wanting to travel.

As a six-year-old, Christie did not know her family spent the year in France as a way to save money. The experience was the beginning of Christie's love of travel, but it was also a more typical, or normal, period in her childhood. Not spending the days isolated at Ashfield, she made friends at the various hotels where they stayed. She also learned how to swim. She played with companions and didn't have to solely depend on her imagination for entertainment.

Education at Ashfield

Christie received her education in multiple ways which would seem nontraditional to American students today. She never attended a local school with other children her age. Primarily, Clara took charge of Christie's education at home. Rumor has it that Clara didn't want to teach Christie to read until she was eight years old. Reading was very important in the Miller household, however, so Christie actually began reading at the age of five, in 1896. Her parents and Madge visited the United States of America, and they sent her many letters written in simple language that she could read. From then on, Christie was encouraged to read nearly everything.

Her father and Madge ended up being Christie's primary writing and spelling teachers. Christie had learned how to read by matching an entire word with its meaning, not by learning letters. Owing to this unorthodox way of learning to read, there is a myth that she had a hard time differentiating between the letters *B* and *R*, and she was a very inconsistent speller. Spelling would remain a challenge for Christie throughout her life, but there is no evidence that it was because of the manner in which she learned how to read.

Frederick also taught her arithmetic, or math, every morning after breakfast. Christie liked the subject very much and took after her father in her ability to quickly complete sums and review tables. She loved solving problems, and in her own words, "found it quite enthralling." She was also exceptionally good at proportions, which served her well when she worked to compound drugs when she worked at the dispensary.

As an adult, Christie would be extremely defensive about her lack of formal education. Her parents and sister taught her reading, writing, and history, but above all else she had to be curious if she wanted to learn. She learned mostly on her own as a child, and she remained an **autodidact** into adulthood. She was naturally curious, and her desire for self-directed learning served her well. Even without much formal education, Christie was able to hold her own with Oxford-educated archaeologists.

Christie's Formal Education

Christie's life expanded and became much more social after Frederick, her father, passed away. In 1902, Christie was sent to Miss Guyer's Girls School in Torquay. There she learned grammar, algebra, and spelling under the tutelage of a woman named Miss Guyer. She attended two days a week. In addition to attending Miss Guyer's school, she also began attending a dance class and making more friends. When she was fifteen years old, her mother rented out Ashfield and the two of them traveled to Paris, where Christie stayed for nearly two years. In Paris, Christie tried out a few different finishing schools, which were establishments that focused on preparing young ladies for society by teaching social graces, from manners and etiquette to fashion and conversation. She attended one called Mademoiselle Cabernet's, which Madge had attended, along with two other schools: Les Marroniers and Miss Dryden's.

Christie loved activities, and she had a gift for pleasure. Almost anything that Christie undertook she enjoyed, especially as a teenager. In Paris, she found enjoyment nearly everywhere. She liked the beauty of the city and being able to purchase her first adult clothing, especially an evening dress to wear to special events. Christie attended the opera with friends for the first time, and she also took classes in painting, dancing, and **deportment**. Christie even had her first crush on a hotel reception clerk.

Music Career

While Christie was in Paris appreciating everything from food to painting, she was most engaged in music. The city afforded Christie the opportunity to take music lessons.

For a while, Christie trained on the piano nearly seven hours a day with a teacher named Charles Furster. Despite the time she devoted to the piano, Christie was not a success. Toward the end of her time in Paris, she gave an informal concert that was nearly catastrophic. Christie was too overwhelmed by her nerves and could not play her pieces well. Performing on the piano was not going to be the way that Christie would fulfill her dream of being a musician. Her musical true love, however, was opera.

Christie's singing was slightly more successful than her attempts on the piano, and she truly loved to sing, especially opera. As a soprano with a clear, strong voice, Christie worked with a prestigious teacher, Monsieur Boué. Unlike when Christie performed on the piano, singing in public allowed her voice to blossom. She thrived on being able to express herself through

At age sixteen, Christie enjoyed her life in Paris, France.

music. After six months of working with Monsieur Boué, she was able to perform **arias**. In 1909, she saw Wagner's *The Ring* with her sister, Madge, and from that moment on she longed to be a professional opera singer. Christie wanted to perform. Unfortunately, when she sang for a friend with connections at the Metropolitan Opera House, Christie was told that she was better suited to being a concert singer, not an opera singer.

Her aspirations to become an opera singer were ultimately set aside. She proudly told her mother that they could be saved the expense of the music lessons. Christie wrote in her autobiography, "I could sing as much as I liked, but there was no point in going on studying singing. I had never really believed that my dream could come true—but it is a good thing to have *had* a dream and to have enjoyed it." As music began to take less of Christie's time, she began to write more and more consistently. Even though Christie would become famous for her writing, it never filled her heart and mind the same way that music did. For Christie, music allowed her to lose herself in beauty in a way she never could when she was writing. At the age of sixty-three, while playing a confessions game, Christie admitted that she would have liked to be an opera singer more than anything else.

Early Writings

Christie did not dream of becoming a career writer, but she did begin writing as a young girl. One of her earliest surviving poems was written and dated April 1901. Another of her early poems was titled "Ode to Christopher Columbus" and was about her cat. Christie's first appearance in print was a poem published in a local newspaper. She also had further poems

Like many young women of her time, Christie desired to be married.

published in the *Poetry Review*, but even so, it was actually Christie's older sister, Madge, who first showed promise as the writer of the family.

Madge published several stories in *Vanity Fair* in 1902. In the 1920s, she also wrote a play that was produced in London's West End called *The Claimant*. While Madge could have also been a writer, after *The Claimant* she only dabbled, writing a few more plays, while Christie was henceforth the writer of the family. Christie's brother, Monty, also wrote, although never for popular consumption. His notebooks were full of unfinished poems, plays, and short stories.

As Christie grew older, she began to write more short stories. In 1908, she wrote a story titled "The House of Beauty" that was published shortly thereafter. The story was a product of her failure to build a career as an opera singer. Clara encouraged Christie to keep writing like her sister. In fact, Christie wrote her stories on Madge's typewriter. She did not, however, sign them as "Agatha Miller" but with various **pseudonyms** like Mack Miller, Nathaniel Miller and Sydney West. Other than "The House of Beauty," Christie's stories weren't being published. Madge had much greater success with her stories as a teenager than Christie did at the time. Even though Christie would ultimately be the family's great success, she would always feel competitive with Madge.

As Christie struggled with having her writing published, she threw herself into a young-adult social life. She attended regattas and other parties in Torquay. She was an extremely attractive young woman who had a gentle confidence. Christie attended events and socialized with the goal of falling in love and meeting someone who could be her husband. Even with her talents in singing and writing, she always wanted to get married and begin her life as a wife. Years later, Christie wrote about that period in her life, saying, "I wasn't sitting and writing. I was going about meeting young men." She was not waiting for life, or a husband to come to her; Christie was out searching for the life she wanted.

Coming of Age

Christie made her debut into society in Cairo, Egypt. Clara and Christie were staying in Cairo because the climate was much better for Clara's health, and the cost of living was more favorable than Torquay for their financial difficulties. Cairo was a popular and economical destination for people of the Millers' social class. They stayed at the Gezirah Palace Hotel, and Christie loved it.

That winter, during the coming out season, there were five dances every week. Christie loved wearing her shimmering, pale-pink satin dress, which she bought special for the events. Over the course of the winter, she met thirty men. In the end, she didn't fall in love or meet her future husband there, but she thoroughly enjoyed her time in Cairo and her introduction to society life. Christie was ready for the next steps of adulthood.

Agatha Christie's Early Romances

Young Agatha Miller desperately wanted to be married. She first met Archie Christie, her future husband, on October 12, 1912, at a dance for young men and women back in England. At the time, it was proper for men to seek a woman to dance with them by signing up on the woman's card. At the dance both attended at Ugbrooke Mansion, Archie signed up for three dances on Agatha's card. After two dances, he asked for

Children's Literature

Christie was a voracious reader. Some of her favorites were by Edith Nesbit and Louisa May Alcott, especially *Little Women. Little Women* focuses on the lives the growing girls of the March family, especially when their father is away at war. The matriarchy in the novel was comforting and inspirational for Christie as she grew up.

Because there were few children's books in circulation, Christie would often read more advanced books. She loved receiving books as gifts. At age eight, she received the famous adventure book *Robinson Crusoe,* by Daniel Defoe, from

Some of Beatrix Potter's famous stories of animals, including *The Tale of Peter Rabbit,* with her original illustrations

her sister, Madge. In addition to *Robinson Crusoe,* Christie read many adventure books, like *Treasure Island,* by Robert Louis Stevenson.

Christie was becoming literate at the same time that a wide range of literature began to become available for children, but she would miss out on some of the advances in children's literature, such as pop-up books and vividly illustrated texts. In 1902, the works of Beatrix Potter began to fill a void with *The Tale of Peter Rabbit.* Potter also provided the illustrations for the books. The next several years brought a series of tales for children about animals in the natural world with human characteristics.

three additional dances. Archie was immediately infatuated with her. She was also drawn to him but did not realize how serious he was until a few days after the gathering. Archie showed up at Ashfield to have tea, and his affection excited her. Clara, however, did not easily like Archie, and she never was truly at ease with the two as a couple.

When the two met, Archie was twenty-three years old, just a year older than Agatha. He was second lieutenant in the Royal Field Artillery. He was ambitious, but he had no money to set up a home or life. As a way to advance his career, he spent £75 (about $9,200 in 2017) on flying lessons. Three months prior to meeting Agatha, he became the 245th qualified aviator in Great Britain.

Agatha and Archie's relationship moved quickly. On January 4, 1913, the two attended a concert together, and Archie insisted and pleaded that she marry him. He was leaving in two days to begin his training with the Royal Flying Corps, and he wanted to be sure of Agatha's feelings before leaving. Agatha did not give him a definitive answer but told her mother about the proposal the next day. The two wouldn't marry for nearly two years, and occasionally during this period they would call the engagement off.

Other Relationships

At the time Archie proposed to Agatha, she was technically engaged to another man, Reggie Lucy. In fact, she had been engaged multiple times by 1913. Agatha was proposed to by two different men she met when she was in Cairo, but neither relationship was serious. Her first earnest proposal was from a man named Colonel Bolston Fletcher. Fletcher courted Agatha with extravagant presents and love letters. Agatha was very flattered and she wondered if she was in love. She felt strong emotions, mainly because she was flattered by the attention. Although she was delighted by his attention, Agatha turned him down.

Agatha's next proposal came from a man named Wilfred Pirie, who was a boring and solemn man, but he had money and status. He did not drink or smoke, and she thought that kissing him was very dull. Agatha was only attracted to the things that he could provide. He was a safe choice. The Pirie family had been friends with the Millers for years, which made him an acceptable choice by cultural standards of the time. Because he was a sub-lieutenant in the Royal Navy, he would be away much of the time, and Agatha could continue living at Ashfield and maintain her relationship with her mother. Clara especially desired this particular engagement and marriage for her daughter. Although Agatha wanted the romance and excitement of engagement and marriage, she was not eager to have her life change substantially for Pirie. In the end, Wilfred Pirie went on an expedition to South America, and Agatha moved on.

Next came Reggie Lucy, the man to whom Agatha was engaged when she met Archie Christie. He was the older brother of some casual friends and a major in the Gunners by profession. Reggie was easy going, and he and Agatha enjoyed relaxed camaraderie and conversation. Clara also liked him and supported the relationship. Reggie proposed when he was home for ten days' leave. In the end, he would not return to Torquay and Devon for two years due to his professional assignment, and he insisted that Agatha consider herself a free woman during the time of his absence. Agatha greatly wanted to be married and didn't want to be considered

Wagner and Music

Richard Wagner was a nineteenth-century German composer primarily known for his operas. He died in 1883, seven years before Christie was born. Wagner was known for writing his own librettos, meaning the text and lyrics, in addition to writing the music for his operas. Most composers of opera did not do this. Beginning in 1849, he also contributed to the reimagining of opera as "music drama," where all musical, poetic, and theatrical elements are fused together, and the orchestra is just as important as the singers. His most famous works include *Tristan and Isolde* and *The Ring of the Nibelung*, a monumental cycle of four operas.

Christie loved the music of Wagner throughout her life. Her love affair began in Paris when she wanted to be an opera singer and saw some of his music performed for the first time. On one of her first dates with Archie Christie, the two of them attended a concert of Wagner's music at the Torquay Pavillion. The evening was magical, and at one point Archie declared that Christie *had* to marry him.

Richard Wagner was Christie's favorite opera composer.

single for two years, so before the couple parted, they were engaged. At that time, she was content to wait.

In the end, why did Agatha pick Archie Christie over Reggie Lucy? In journals and reflections when she was older, Agatha did not argue that Archie was a kinder man or that he had more money or was more attractive. In fact, it took a while for Agatha, despite saying she would marry Archie, to truly give in, and she did write to Reggie Lucy to formally break off the engagement. There were times where Archie wanted to call the marriage off and thought it would be impossible. Agatha's mother, Clara, also had misgivings, but Agatha had decided Archie was the one. Finally, on Christmas Eve 1914, they were married.

three

Christie Embraces Adulthood

"The lure of the past came up to grab me. To see a dagger slowly appearing ... The carefulness of lifting pots and objects from the soil filled me with a longing to be an archaeologist myself." —Agatha Christie

Throughout Christie's childhood, she dreamed of marriage and life as a married woman. Along the way, she considered being an opera singer, and she worked hard to begin writing, but adulthood was tied, in Christie's mind, to marriage. When she made the decision

Opposite: Agatha Christie walks with her first husband, Archie Christie, in 1919.

to marry Archie, she was making a decision to live as an adult and leave behind the multiple marriage proposals and parties. It is safe to assume her life did not turn out as she envisioned while playing with her imaginary friends as a young girl at Ashfield.

Agatha and Archie Christie

As discussed, Christie was desperate to marry, and she chose Archie Christie as her husband. She wanted a conventional marriage, but Archie was not the conventional choice. Bolton Fletcher, Wilfred Pirie, and Reggie Lucy all would have been more stable choices in hindsight. The Miller family and the Christie family did not know each other at all, and in early twentieth-century aristocratic England, the families of a young couple nearly always knew each other.

Christie saw the fulfillment of all her practical and romantic dreams in her marriage to Archie. Yet Archie was also moody and strangely vulnerable. All Archie's characteristics, both negative and positive, helped Christie's imagination run wild, and she built up marriage to Archie as nothing but fantasy. She was extremely attracted to Archie, and the excitement of the on-and-off-again relationship felt romantic to her. Christie thought that once the two were married, all of the practicalities would follow. She desired all the little pieces of companionship that marriage brings, like setting up a household and having dinner together. She felt that these would come easily once the two of them were committed to each other. The resistance of Clara to the match only resulted in Christie's desire to marry Archie with more enthusiasm.

The Couple During World War I

On August 3, 1914, Christie and her mother took a train journey to Salisbury, England, to say goodbye to Archie, who was leaving for France nine days later. Christie wrote about her parting with Archie, describing the tears and the dread at the final departure, but she also moved on and tried to fill her time with activities while he was gone.

Christie was extremely pragmatic and acknowledged that her life had changed drastically, both in regards to the war and her relationship with Archie. She didn't dwell on the changes but threw herself into something new to occupy her time: nursing with the VAD. As a nurse, she cleaned the hospital and assisted in some gruesome surgeries. She wrote in her journal about how she started shaking uncontrollably when she attended her first surgery, but she did not discuss the emotional effects of the trauma she had seen. Christie had a disposition that enabled her to be an excellent nurse: she was efficient, kind, and detached. She didn't write about all of the carnage and death. Christie did not seem overwhelmed by the despair of war, either. Somehow she made the transition from innocent young woman, ignorant of most political and worldly affairs, to a wise wartime nurse.

The Christies' Marriage

In the midst of her new life as a nurse, Christie finally became a wife. Shortly after the wedding on Christmas Eve 1914, Archie returned to France and to fighting in the war. The couple was not able to begin their lives together in the way that Christie imagined. Although the two were separated as newlyweds and during the first four years of their marriage, the war times were almost easier for them than the subsequent years.

The Christies' early marriage had its challenges; the main two were having enough money and finding adequate employment. Archie did not desire a career in the military, and so he left the army after the war. The couple settled in a flat in London. Postwar England had few job opportunities, and the economy was not robust. He was often depressed because he found it difficult to find employment. They did not have a maid, so Agatha cooked and cleaned. She tried to be the perfect domestic partner instead of writing or trying to find work herself. Even though times were tough, Christie enjoyed the early marriage because she was able to act out the way she thought a marriage should be. They depended on each other, and in that way, Christie had achieved her ideal marriage.

Shortly after the war ended, Christie discovered that she was pregnant. In 1919, Christie gave birth at Ashfield to her daughter, Rosalind Margaret. She loved her daughter, but she would never be devoted to Rosalind the same way she was to her own mother, Clara. Christie had no qualms about leaving Rosalind to travel the world or sending her to boarding school at the age of nine. Christie also worried that having Rosalind would change her relationship with Archie.

Unfortunately, other forces eventually impacted the couple. As the years went by and they became more financially secure, they grew apart. Christie started to spend a large amount of her time working on her writing, but she still desired Archie's companionship. Archie, on the other hand, when not working, spent a great amount of his leisure time golfing. Golf was his favorite pastime, but his wife had little interest in the sport.

The British Empire Exhibition Tour

For Christie, one of the highest points of her first marriage was the world tour she completed together with her husband. In 1922, a friend of Archie's who worked for the government was going to sail around the world to visit all of the countries in the British Empire for the upcoming British Empire Exhibition. This friend asked Archie to come along as a financial advisor. Archie agreed, although it turned out that he was inaccurately guaranteed a job upon his return. Clara and Madge offered to care for Rosalind, and the couple set off on the trip.

Despite a bout with seasickness, Christie loved nearly every minute of her almost year-long trip. On the circuit, they visited South Africa, several other African countries and Victoria Falls, India, China, Australia, and Canada. They returned to England via New York. It was Christie's first visit to the United States.

In Cape Town, South Africa, Christie became the first British woman to surf standing up. She also learned, while in Cape

A paddle steamer ship, similar to what Christie would have traveled on while she was in Africa with Archie

Town, that her second novel, *The Secret Adversary*, was to be published.

The Empire Tour was a turning point for Christie. She was able to fulfill her desire to travel, and it provided her a wealth of experiences that she would draw on as she wrote more consistently. Christie's time traveling with Archie would also awaken her interest in archaeology. She enjoyed visiting archaeological museums as she visited various sites and wrote to her mother about how spending an afternoon looking at human skulls was one of the best afternoons of her life.

Regrettably, the trip had a negative effect on the Christie family's finances. Archie's job had not been saved for him, and the employment situation in England was getting worse. It took Archie quite a while to find a new job. In the interim, it was up to Christie to make up some of the income, and so she wrote *The Man in the Brown Suit*. The novel was inspired by her time in Pretoria, South Africa. It contained themes that she would use again and again, conspiracy and money, and was set in South Africa.

Over time, Christie's writing helped her and Archie gain some more financial security. The *Evening News*, an English publication, offered Christie £500 (about $30,600 in 2017) for the **serial** rights to *The Man in the Brown Suit*. With the money, Christie bought a car. She felt freedom in being able to buy the car and being financially secure, yet she was still comfortably married. The car itself also allowed her to move about freely. Although Christie greatly prized her marriage, her own freedom and mobility was equally as important.

The End of the Christies' Marriage

Christie and her husband's relationship was put under duress by the death of Christie's beloved mother, Clara, at the beginning of 1926. All of the death and dying Christie had come into contact with during the war could not prepare her for the death of her greatest confidant. Archie had struggled with the closeness of his wife's relationship with her mother, and when Clara passed, Christie did not see him as properly sympathetic. Archie was out of town when Clara died, and when he returned to be with a grief-stricken Christie, he comforted her by suggesting they go on a trip to Spain. Christie was offended by the suggestion, but Archie only suggested the trip as a distraction. In Christie's grief, the suggestion of a trip to Spain became a point of contention. Years later, Christie blamed herself for being too frustrated with Archie while she was grieving.

The death of her mother didn't just put a strain on Christie's marriage and her relationship with Archie, but also on her ability to write and do work. She was in charge of settling her mother's estate and cleaning up and sorting through Ashfield, the Miller family home. Ashfield had been falling into disrepair. The smart thing to do would have been to sell it, but Christie was too emotionally attached to the property, despite its financial burden.

Christie continued to face challenges after her mother's death. Today, she might have been diagnosed with depression. She was sleeping badly and eating erratic meals. Christie would even occasionally forget who or where she was. During this stretch of poor mental health, Archie also admitted to Christie that he had fallen in love with another woman named Nancy Neele, whom he played golf with, and asked for a divorce.

A Mysterious Disappearance

In 1926, not long after Archie confessed to loving someone else, Christie disappeared. Today, there are still various theories about how and why Agatha Christie abandoned her car and disappeared on December 3. The public was extremely concerned for Christie. Rewards were offered, and thousands of police officers and volunteers combed the countryside. Even airplanes were involved in the search. She was found eleven days later, on December 14, at the Harrogate Old Swan Hotel under the name Mrs. Teresa Neele.

Writers and researchers interested in Agatha Christie still are not sure of the exact order of events to Christie's disappearance. Most sources do agree that on December 3, Christie drove away from the Christie home in Sunningdale, England, called "Styles." She left a note stating that she was going to Yorkshire. From there, it seems her state of mind changed drastically: she could make decisions but was not mentally present as herself. Christie's grief over her mother's death and knowledge of Archie's changing affections likely played a role in what occurred.

The press at the time followed her vanishing almost like the modern-day tabloids, including the dissemination of misinformation. Reporters and critics alike thought it was a publicity stunt to sell more books, or possibly to embarrass Archie. Even years later, the 1979 film *Agatha* and Jared Cade's 1998 book, *Agatha Christie and the Eleven Missing Days*, would attempt to tell the story of what happened. Those are just two out of many works that speculate about Christie's

Christie poses for the camera, circa 1926.

disappearance in 1926, although Christie herself did not write about it in her autobiography.

Once Christie was found, stress for her continued. She was diagnosed with amnesia and underwent treatment for her mental health, all the while not knowing what would happen to her marriage, where she would live, or how it would affect Rosalind. Christie also owed her publishers a book, which she badly wanted to deliver on because she needed the money. However, she felt completely uninspired and unable to write. Fifteen years later, as a result of this time, Christie would ask her agent to hold a manuscript of hers in reserve so that she would never again have to write simply for the money. She did not like being put in that position.

Divorce from Archie

The Christies finally divorced in 1928. Agatha retained custody of Rosalind and moved to London. In late 1928 and 1929, she wrote a variety of short stories which she then sold to various magazines. She paid her bills with the proceeds from her next two books, *The Seven Dials Mystery* and *Partners in Crime*. She also began writing a series of novels under the pseudonym Mary Westmacott. All of those works were written during a very lonely, difficult time. When she was married, she socialized with Archie and their friends. Many of her London friends were married. Mingling was often a couples' affair, and she felt like the odd person out.

As her main ambition up to this point had been to be a wife, she was deeply devastated when her marriage to Archie ended. She had been brought up to believe that marriage was the most important thing for a woman. For a while, Christie felt a lot of guilt about the divorce, even though Archie was the one who fell for someone else and requested the divorce. At first, Christie hoped beyond reason that Archie might come back to her and Rosalind, and that they might be a happy family again. Realistically, Christie knew that would never happen. She accepted the divorce and carried the guilt of a failed marriage with her throughout her life.

In many ways, Christie's personality changed after the divorce. She began to write more seriously and earnestly than before. She also had a new kind of freedom, one she did not necessarily want but that she took advantage of. Christie did not have to live up to what was expected of a housewife. She did not have to focus on being slim, feminine, and pleasing, although Archie often gave her a hard time about her weight. As a result, she threw herself into writing and travel, two things that she couldn't always freely pursue when she was married to Archie.

In the end, Christie would live a far more successful life than she would have had if she stayed married to Archie. She became one of the most famous women in the world. She bought multiple houses and traveled freely to exotic lands. Christie married again, to a man that respected her intellect. Although Christie would always mourn her first marriage, she did rebuild a new and extremely successful life.

Travel and a New Life

As Christie adjusted to life without Archie, she realized how different the two of them were. Archie was content to travel the English countryside and find new golf courses. Christie, however, craved worldwide travel and seeing unknown sights. Christie liked experiencing new things. Although she certainly had not initially wanted the independence the divorce provided, she ultimately embraced her new life. She began to write and to travel by herself.

In 1928, Christie booked a ticket to the West Indies. She was looking forward to leaving a cold winter and spending time in a sunny, tropical climate. As luck would have it, a day or two before she was due to depart, Christie attended a dinner party and sat next to a man who had just returned from traveling to Baghdad, Iraq. She had always wanted to travel to Baghdad, and he provided her with lots of information, including how to travel by train on the Orient Express. He also

Police reconstruct the site where Christie abandoned her car and disappeared in 1926.

told Christie she could see an archaeological dig at Ur, which was famous at the time for allegedly being the site of the biblical flood. The next morning, Christie decided to change her trip and head to Baghdad. Friends and family protested that it was unsafe for a woman to travel unaccompanied to the Middle East, but Christie was excited and felt ready for a new adventure.

She spent time in Baghdad, and then at the archaeological dig site in Ur. Her writing fame preceded her, and Leonard Woolley and his wife, Katherine, welcomed her onto the dig site. The Woolleys were both famous archaeologists. Christie returned to Ur in 1930 as a friend of the Woolleys and a member of the expedition team. She was becoming an archaeologist, not just a traveler and observer.

Life with Max Mallowan

During the 1930 Ur site dig, Christie met a young man—just twenty-five years old—named Max Mallowan. Mallowan gave Christie a tour of local sights between Ur and Baghdad, and a friendship between the two began. Christie felt comfortable with Mallowan from the very start. Because of the age difference, she did not consider him as a potential love interest and thought nothing of the relationship. Christie and Mallowan, along with the Woolleys, were traveling through Greece when Christie received a **telegram** stating Rosalind was extremely ill with pneumonia. Mallowan decided to accompany Christie back to England so she would not have to make the four-day journey alone. After Mallowan supported Christie on the trip back to England, the friendship evolved, and the two became a couple.

After the journey, Mallowan and Christie spent time together in London. When they weren't in the city together, the two corresponded frequently. After a long talk one evening, Mallowan declared that he believed one day Christie would marry him. Despite all the trauma from the ending of her first marriage, Christie was excited by this idea, even with their fourteen-year age difference.

Mallowan provided emotional support to Christie, much in the same way that her mother, Clara, did. She felt safe with Mallowan. Furthermore, the extreme age difference, among

Christie and Max Mallowan, her second husband, before traveling to Iraq together for a dig in 1933

Divorce

Archie and Agatha Christie divorced in 1928, but divorce was not a common practice in England. Changes had begun in 1909 when a Royal Commission examined the divorce laws. The commission found lots of inconsistency in the law and how it was applied, with it being especially unfair to women seeking a divorce. The Royal Commission recommended more simplified and cost-efficient processes for divorce, but nothing was immediately done. The increase in divorces after World War I, coupled with some women being enfranchised for the first time, led to changes. In 1923, the Matrimonial Causes Bill allowed adultery as a sole cause for divorce. A woman no longer had to prove additional faults against her husband. In 1925, the Summary Jurisdiction (Separation and Maintenance) Act further extended the reasons either partner could request a divorce.

other differences, made Christie's relationship with Mallowan decidedly different from her relationship with Archie. Their shared interests in travel and archaeology made them excellent companions.

On September 11, 1930, in Scotland, Mallowan and Christie were married. They honeymooned in Venice. At the beginning of the marriage, Christie vowed that she would never neglect Mallowan, still blaming herself for the dissolution of her first marriage. Mallowan was to return to the Woolleys' dig, and Christie kept a home in London and a house in Wallingford. Because she was reluctant to leave Mallowan's side, she began an annual writing and traveling routine, spending about six months every year with him in the Middle East.

Christie the Archaeologist

The ten years prior to World War II were a very good period in Christie's life. In that time, she went on her first archaeological dig and later began accompanying Mallowan on digs regularly. On the excavation site, Christie had many tasks, including photographing and cataloging many of the recovered artifacts. She returned to Ur, the site where she had met Mallowan, one more time in 1931. On a 1932 dig at Arpachiyha, near Ninevah in Iraq, Christie was responsible for keeping a written record and helping to reassemble pottery fragments. From there, Mallowan was given his own dig—which was a major career goal—at Arpachiyha. He excavated there for one year, and Christie provided the drawings. During this period of her life, Christie wrote that she was "bursting with happiness." In 1935, the couple decided to move to Chagar Bazar, Syria, for the next few years.

Living in the Middle East

Christie greatly enjoyed her time in Chagar Bazar, Syria. The conditions were often extremely uncomfortable and grueling, but they were a challenge that she accepted. Her time in prewar Syria was unique and important enough that she chronicled it in a memoir titled *Come, Tell Me How You Live*. Much of the memoir included all of the challenges of living in the desert, like finding accommodation and enduring terrible heat, but all of the challenges were explained with good humor and with the backdrop of her love of archaeology. Some critics have argued that *Come, Tell Me How You Live* is too cheerful and that Christie wrote the memoir solely to impress Mallowan with how much she was enjoying archaeology and being at the dig sites.

Regardless of the tone of *Come, Tell Me How You Live*, Christie had a genuine love of the East, the archaeological dig sites, and many of Mallowan's colleagues. The dig sites also allowed Christie to escape her life in England every year. Edmund Cork, Christie's publisher, constantly was responding to press inquiries about Christie that she was in Syria/Iraq. Luckily for Christie, Cork was an excellent manager and was able to protect her interests and manage her affairs while she was out of the country.

Spending time at the archaeological digs fascinated Christie, and her adventurous travels to the sites also provided her with wonderful inspiration for her writings. By the time Christie was in her forties, she was constantly producing new works and was well received by critics and the reading public. She could write while traveling, and she enjoyed being with Mallowan. In 1933, Christie completed two detective stories, two collections of short stories, and a Mary Westmacott novel, *Unfinished Portrait*. Even though Christie was well suited to life with Mallowan at archaeological dig sites, *Unfinished Portrait* illustrates that anxieties from her first marriage and life with Archie remained.

The travel to the Middle East allowed Christie the adventure that she had craved and never achieved when she was married to Archie. She fell into a pattern where she would summer in England with Rosalind, and the winters were spent at the dig sites. Christie wrote consistently as well, producing two or three books per year.

Even at sixty years of age, Christie continued going with Mallowan on archaeological digs. In fact, the time in the desert during the English winter helped Christie stay healthy. The work with Mallowan continued to suit her as she aged, archaeological work being so similar to detection. Working as an archaeologist, she needed to recognize and organize clues with the few pieces of evidence uncovered to reconstruct what might have happened. Today, few people associate her name with her archaeological pedigree, but Christie lived an amazing life making contributions to the field. Artifacts likely cleaned with her face cream are among the finest collection of ancient ivories ever found, according to John Curtis, who was keeper of the Middle East collections at the British Museum in 2011.

Finding a Home

Although the 1930s were a golden period in many ways for Christie, the decade ended with some personal sadness. First, in 1938, Christie's beloved dog, Peter, died. She greatly admired goodness and loyalty in dogs, and the death of Peter, to whom she had dedicated two books, was hard for her. Also that same year, Christie made the decision to sell Ashfield, the family home.

For many years, Christie refused to part with Ashfield, even when it would have made financial sense to sell it. Early in their marriage, Mallowan stated that he liked Ashfield. Christie, however, recognized that Mallowan was uncomfortable with all the heavy family memories of the house. Christie decided to sell Ashfield for a variety of reasons. Torquay had become more developed. The fields that she loved as a child were now housing developments. In addition, she barely knew anyone who lived there. Christie recognized that it was the right time to sell the house, but she would always miss Ashfield. Nearly five years after its sale, she wrote to Mallowan that she felt homeless. When it was demolished in the 1960s, she cried.

Even though Christie wrote dramatically that she felt homeless, Christie was never without a home. She and Mallowan made a home when they were in England at Winterbrook in Wallingford early in their marriage. She bought the elegant, yet homey, property in 1934. It had an excellent garden that stretched out to the Thames River. However nice Winterbrook was, it was not Ashfield, nor was it the house of Christie's dreams. Greenway House became that home when she purchased it in 1938. Christie would be at home at Greenway when World War II began. She owned the property until the end of her life. The home had room for Rosalind and her family as well as for visitors and guests. In much the same way Christie took care of Ashfield for Clara, her daughter Rosalind and her family would become the caretakers of Greenway. Greenway was almost as beloved to Christie as Ashfield had been.

War, Again

As World War II broke out, the golden period of Christie's life came to a close. Mallowan obtained a job in Cairo assisting with the war effort with his language skills, and the couple was separated. Christie stayed in England and continued writing while also volunteering at the dispensary at the University College Hospital of London, much as she did during World War I. This time, however, Christie was much older, and the seven-hour days were a bit more of a struggle for her. She left the hospital exhausted each day.

Christie also struggled with a little bit of depression during this time. She was run down from her time in the dispensary, and she missed Mallowan terribly. Their relationship was maintained mainly through letters for the three years they were separated. Christie wrote a lot about shared experiences and memories. She was feeling anxious during their time apart, and her fears about another marriage failing haunted her.

The World War II years did hold some joy for Christie. In the midst of the war, Christie also became a grandmother. On September 21, 1943, Rosalind gave birth to a son, Matthew. Despite her reserve as a mother, Christie became a doting grandmother and spent a lot of time helping to care for Matthew, especially during the war years.

The Later Years

After the war ended and Christie was reunited with Mallowan, her pace began to slow for the first time in her life. While she may have slowed down, she still wrote a number of detective novels each year. Her work began to be serialized for radio

Cars and Automobiles

Throughout Agatha Christie's lifetime, cars became increasingly popular. They grew in popularity from a new invention and a novelty to the main mode of transportation used by most people. Although there are various definitions for the first car or automobile, it is generally agreed that the first modern car was invented in 1886 by Karl Benz—just four years before Christie's birth.

Cars were not immediately mass-produced and available to the public in the 1890s. The first mass-produced automobile was the Model T, which was manufactured by Ford Motor Company beginning in 1908 until 1927. Car usage grew much quicker in the United States than it did in Western Europe, but

A 1924 Model T automobile

the Model T was eventually produced in England and Europe, in addition to the United States, and its popularity grew. The Model T's popularity was in part due to its cost. Due to Henry Ford's invention of the assembly line, the Model T only cost $300 by 1927. Even though Christie didn't buy a Model T, the £500 she received for *The Man in the Brown Suit* was adequate to purchase a car.

and television. Christie began to focus more of her attention on writing plays, although she was less successful as a playwright than as a detective novelist.

Christie prioritzed enjoying her life from middle age on. She and Mallowan traveled, both together and separately. She saw places like India, Pakistan, Sri Lanka, and Turkey. Christie attended concerts of her beloved Wagner and the coronation of Queen Elizabeth II. She was as social as she wanted to be and yet thoroughly enjoyed her time at home at Greenway, gardening and writing.

Once Christie hit the 1970s, she seemed to begin aging much more quickly. She had a hip operation, and she had to spend some time learning to walk again. Some of her final outings were the premiere of the movie version of her book *Murder on the Orient Express*, and an annual party for her play *The Mousetrap* in 1974. On January 12, 1976, Agatha Christie passed away.

four

The Great Detective Novel

"Beware! Peril to the detective who says: 'It is so small—it does not matter. It will not agree. I will forget it.' That way lies confusion! Everything matters." —Hercule Poirot

Agatha Christie, approximately thirty years into her writing career, was still reluctant to identify herself as a professional writer. As late as the 1950s, she was quoted as saying, "Nothing in my life surprised me more than

Opposite: Christie in 1946, posing at her typewriter, which she did not generally use to write her novels

success as a writer." Even though Christie was amazed by her success, to an outside observer she may have appeared to be on the path to becoming a writer at an early age, through the encouragement of her family. Christie dabbled in writing and had several unpublished poems, plays, and shorts stories already written when she began her first manuscript for publication. She wrote her first serious piece of detective fiction in 1912, at the age of twenty-two, after a bet with her sister. Madge bet Christie that she could not write a detective story, and she rose to the challenge.

During World War I, Christie had time to herself because Archie was away fighting in the war. Her extra time, the goading of her sister, her ability to write, and her new knowledge of poisons and experience as a medical dispenser helped her to complete her first detective novel, *The Mysterious Affair at Styles*. Without knowing it, Christie jump-started a groundbreaking career as she sent out the manuscript for her first detective novel.

Christie's most well-known and celebrated skill was her talent to write detective novels. Her ability to craft methodical, formulaic mysteries was an exceptional strength. She also had a hunger for knowledge, and her desire to learn and expand her experience helped her create colorful worlds for her readers. Christie's immense body of work can best be understood through her technique and process, her life, and the famous characters she created.

The Agatha Christie Formula

While Christie's detective novels nearly all center on a murder, the text never describes the actual crime taking place. The death itself is not shocking, gory, or gruesome. It is the mystery, the task of finding out who committed the murder, which is the most important task of the novel. The killings do not attempt to tug at the heartstrings of readers or invoke sentiment. For example, in *The Mysterious Affair at Styles*, the victim is not a character the reader necessarily loves or identifies with. As a writer, Christie was not trying to convince the reader to feel sympathy for a beloved character who has been unjustly murdered. Instead, the audience is supposed to participate, and to rationally try to figure out who committed the murder and why. They key to the detective novel, for Christie, was not to rile the emotions of the reader but rather to encourage her audience to review the accumulation of evidence in the text and make a rational deduction about who committed the murder. Readers came to recognize what they would get out of an Agatha Christie detective story, and by the 1940s, they kept coming back to the books for the same formula.

The Writing Process

Agatha Christie wrote about the world she knew. Nearly every detective novel she wrote included upper-middle-class families like her own, and English society. In novels set outside of England, Christie used other places that she was familiar with. *Murder on the Orient Express* takes place on a train from the Middle East that Christie had previously traveled on. Similarly, *A Caribbean Mystery*, another novel, grew out of the time that Christie spent in Saint Lucia. When characters and settings weren't traditionally English, they were inspired by something else that Christie had experience with.

Everyday life and ordinary people inspired Christie. Ideas for plots and characters came from observing life around her. For example, her second novel, *The Secret Adversary*, was sparked by a conversation she overheard in a café. The name "Jane Fish" was mentioned at a nearby table, and her imagination took off. She decided the name could be the source of a mystery, and from that moment the plot for a Tommy and Tuppence mystery slowly came alive.

Inspiration could strike at any time, and most of Christie's narrative plots came together through notes. Christie kept hundreds of notebooks throughout her life. She would jot down plot points and character names as they came to her. In the surviving journals, the notes are rather erratic and lack a formula. She didn't create any kind of outline. This is interesting because Christie was so very methodical in her plots; small pieces of evidence slowly accumulate and build upon each other, leading to the solution. Christie's ability to write complex mystery story lines is even more admirable without signs of outlines.

When it came to creating the novels, Christie did not actually do the physical act of writing or typing once she was an established author. Instead, Christie would dictate the works into a **Dictaphone**, and then a secretary would be hired to type out what she had said. When she was writing regularly, a book would take Christie a few months to write, followed by another month of revising before it was sent to her publisher.

Writing in the 1920s

Christie's writing career evolved in the 1920s, and during that time she wrote more than the detective novels she would become famous for. Her first detective novel, *The Mysterious Affair at Styles*, was written in 1916, and she began to learn about

Christie's first detective novel features Hercule Poirot.

business relationships with publishers as she worked toward its eventual publication in 1920. During this decade, Christie published nine novels, and only four of those novels qualify as standard detective novels. Even with these accomplishments, Christie's primary focus was being a wife, not an author. The works were written and submitted as Christie found time, or as her and Archie's finances dwindled and she needed to earn money.

The Mysterious Affair at Styles

Upon its completion, Christie sent the manuscript for *The Mysterious Affair at Styles* out to multiple publishers, and the book was rejected by all of them. She eventually decided to send it to one more publisher, The Bodley Head, in 1918. World War I ended shortly after Christie sent out the manuscript, and Archie came home. Christie gave birth to Rosalind and completely forgot about the novel. Then one day in 1920, she received a letter from The Bodley Head expressing interest in her manuscript.

The publisher was interested in her detective novel, but with a few minor changes and one major change, which included rewriting the final courtroom scene. Christie revised the final courtroom scene, and thus began the tradition of "Poirot reveals all," which would be part her future Poirot novels. In addition to reworking the ending, Christie accepted all of the conditions that The Bodley Head presented her. Under the contract, she would not receive any royalties unless more than two thousand copies of the book were sold. In addition, she had to split any profits from serialization, and The Bodley Head was granted the rights to publish her next five books.

Christie accepted the terms because she was excited to see her novel published, and she had no intention of writing more, especially five more novels. In the end, *The Mysterious Affair at Styles* sold under two thousand copies, so Christie never received any royalties while she was under contract. She did receive £25 of the £50 (about $1,080 out of $2,160 in 2017) offered to her by a magazine for the novel's serialization, per her contract. It is important to note that, after her experience with The Bodley Head, Christie would not easily acquiesce to future demands from a publisher.

The novel, *The Mysterious Affair at Styles*, is a great first detective novel. It introduces many of the themes and ideas that Agatha Christie would use through her other works, including the use of a familiar geographical and social setting. The story takes place in Styles St. Mary, a fictional English village. Christie also utilized the current conditions of the time, World War I

England. Nuances of the wartime climate appear throughout the text and are reinforced with mentions of the rationing of food and the presence of refugees.

The great success of *The Mysterious Affair at Styles* is the plot and the introduction of the detective Hercule Poirot. Both the tightly worked out mystery and the detective who cunningly solves the crime became staples of Christie's work. Although the novel did not earn Christie much money, the legacy and traditions that were established in her very first novel proved to be priceless.

Writing for a Living

Even though Christie was quite pleased with herself and the publication of just one novel, circumstances dictated she write another one. In 1921, her mother's finances were getting worse, and Clara Miller was contemplating selling Christie's beloved childhood home. Christie did not want Ashfield to be sold, and Archie suggested that she write another book. After giving it some thought, Christie began writing again, and her second novel, *The Secret Adversary*, came to fruition. The publisher, The Bodley Head, did not like the text but published it anyway in 1922. The proceeds helped finance Christie's mother staying at Ashfield.

From that point on, the detective novels began to come easily for Christie. In 1923, The Bodley Head published Agatha Christie's *Murder on the Links*. This novel was more similar to *The Mysterious Affair at Styles* as it featured the detective Hercule Poirot and his friend, Hastings, and the publisher liked it a lot more. Christie's next novel, *The Man in the Brown Suit*, grew out of her trip to South Africa and around the world. When she and Archie returned from the Empire Tour, Archie no longer had a job. Christie decided to write the novel to help make money until he found employment. The Bodley Head did not like *The Man in the Brown Suit*, but published it anyway in 1924. The next novel she wrote was rejected by the publisher. She quickly wrote another novel to be published in 1925, *The Secret of Chimneys*, and she was finally able to terminate her relationship with The Bodley Head.

Collins, a different publishing company, became Christie's new publisher after she signed a three-book contract with them in 1924. The two parties worked much better together than Christie and The Bodley Head had. Edmund Cork managed Agatha Christie's work for the publisher and acted as her agent. Both Collins and Cork maintained their relationship with Christie until her death in 1976.

The Murder of Roger Ackroyd, which critics often refer to as her first masterpiece, was her first detective novel published by Collins, in 1926, and it made Agatha Christie a household name. Unfortunately, at the same time Christie was becoming a household name, her husband Archie wanted a divorce.

Their divorce led to some writing challenges for Christie, but she urgently needed to write to fulfill her contract and make money. In 1927, *The Big Four* was published, and the next year, in 1928, came *The Mystery of the Blue Train.* Neither book was well loved by readers, and in later years Christie would describe *The Mystery of the Blue Train* as her all-time worst novel. She wrote both books to pay bills at a time when she was not mentally healthy.

Writings in the 1930s

The decade after Christie's divorce was one of great productivity and focus, and one of the best periods for her writing. From 1930 to 1939, Christie wrote seventeen full-length novels, and nearly every one can be seen as a masterpiece. Agatha Christie's Belgian detective, Hercule Poirot, appeared in twelve of seventeen novels published in the 1930s. It was the golden age of Detective Hercule Poirot. The novels Christie produced were well-constructed mysteries, similar to her famous *The Murder of Roger Ackroyd.* She ended a great decade of writing in 1939 with the publication of *And Then There Were None,* which might be her best-known mystery story.

During this time, Christie's life revolved around her new husband, Max Mallowan. She tried to devote as much time as possible to her husband because she didn't want her second marriage to fail. Christie joked that she threw herself so thoroughly into her marriage that she didn't even remember the books she wrote between 1929 and 1939. Even with her devotion to Mallowan, she had a very successful decade of writing. Mallowan supported Christie's writing endeavors, and so she was able to prioritize both her writing and her marriage.

Evolution

The complexities in Christie's work grew. **Psychology** began to be featured as a science in her novels, like in the 1935 *The A.B.C. Murders.* In addition to the appearance of psychology, Christie's ability to create in-depth characters also grew greatly during the 1930s. Not only was she a more mature human being and writer, but her characters were more mature as well. The

1933 novel *Thirteen at Dinner*, also called *Lord Edgware Dies*, is often held out as the text with the most well defined characters.

Her early novels were often criticized for their elevation of British culture and negative stereotypes of characters from other countries. In the 1930s, this decreased, although a lot of the servants continued to carry ethnic stereotypes. For example, comments seen as anti-Semitic remarks no longer appeared in Christie's novels by the end of the decade. It is not a surprise that stereotypes began to diminish in Christie's work. When she wrote her first novel, she was just twenty-five years old, newly married, and not knowledgeable about the world. In 1939, she was forty-nine and almost ten years into her second marriage. She had traveled much more extensively and had a richer and more complex cultural experience to draw on than she did when she was young. The complexity of characters and plots simply followed the trajectory of her life.

Writings in the 1940s

By the time the 1940s rolled around, Christie wanted to break out of the detective novel and create more "serious" fiction. Christie again wrote under her pseudonym, Mary Westmacott. In general, her Westmacott books and other serious novels did not impress either publishers or critics. The detective novels she did write, like *The Moving Finger*, *Murder in Retrospect* (also called *Five Little Pigs*), *Remembered Death* (also called *Sparkling Cyanide*), *Murder After Hours* (also called *The Hollow*), and *There Is a Tide* (also called *Taken at the Flood*), featured very serious relationships between characters. Her detective novels of this decade generally lack the light-hearted tone of her earlier novels. Hercule Poirot,

Christie celebrates the success of *The Mousetrap* with friends and associates.

who brought a wittiness to many of the detective stories, only appears in six of the thirteen novels Christie published during the 1940s.

Christie also began writing more plays during this time. One of them became greatly successful, *The Mousetrap*. Originally conceived as a script for a twenty-minute **radio play** and later adapted into a full-length theatrical play, *The Mousetrap* is a murder mystery with a surprise-twist ending. Traditionally, the audience members were asked not to reveal the ending when discussing the play. *The Mousetrap* opened in London's West End in 1952 and is still running as of this writing (January 2017), making it the longest-running play of all time.

Christie's writing continued to advance in the 1940s. The greatest change evident in her work was her ability to create rounder, more lifelike characters in her novels. Many of her early novels only included physical descriptions of the characters, not nuances of their personalities. Christie also added more complex themes to her writing. She was wrestling with thoughts about love, marriage, and infidelity, and these themes appear in novels like *Sad Cypress* and *Murder After Hours*. Parenting was also on Christie's mind, specifically mother-daughter relationships. *Evil Under the Sun, The Moving Finger, and Murder After Hours* all present unique and/or problematic mother-daughter relationships.

Writings in the 1950s and Beyond

The traditional detective novels Christie was popular for returned in the 1950s. She refocused on the crime committed and less on the characters, much like many of her early novels. Critics have argued that the quality of Christie's work began to decline in the 1950s. Decline might be too strong of a word, because she continued to produce entertaining and well-written detective novels. Christie's *Ordeal by Innocence* and *Cat Among the Pigeons* are detective novels with excellent character development.

New Themes

Christie also tackled social issues, and the changes in British society, subtly in her texts. In the 1950s, many of her works dealt with changes like the decline of servants. Christie, as a child, had been very attached to the family's servants and counted them almost as family members. In the novel *A Murder is Announced*, only two families in the entire village still have a live-in cook/housemaid. The servant class was disappearing, and upper-middle-class families were no longer as wealthy as they once were owing to lower investment incomes. Great Britain as a country became less prominent in world politics as well. This, as well as the growing number of immigrants and concern regarding Communists, also appears in various ways in Christie's novels.

A new premise also emerged in Christie's texts, one that readers were not receptive to. Beginning with her 1949 novel *Crooked House*, Christie began to assert that character traits are inherited and not shaped by education. More simply, in the nature versus nurture debate, Christie was coming down solidly on the side of nature. This idea reappears in the 1952 novel *Murder with Mirrors* (also called *They Do It with Mirrors*), in which the text argues that a bad environment could not be the reason someone becomes a juvenile delinquent. Christie makes her most fervent point in the 1958 *Ordeal by Innocence*, where the text argues that education and upbringing have little influence in shaping children and their character traits. The novel itself was supposed to be light fiction, but there was a strong preaching tone regarding upbringing. Christie likely felt a lot of guilt as she aged about her hands-off parenting style and the time she spent away from her daughter, Rosalind. By arguing, through her work, that children inherited their traits and were ordained to be of a certain personality, she relieved herself of any guilt and responsibility.

1960s and 1970s

Although there is debate over the quality of Christie's work in the 1950s, there is almost unanimous agreement that the caliber of her novels did decline in the 1960s. Some critics even recommend ignoring the works she wrote in the 1960s, most especially if you are a new reader of Christie's work. They maintain that these are enjoyable if a reader is already attached to certain characters, like Miss Marple. If so, then a reader would likely enjoy *The Mirror Crack'd* or *At Bertram's Hotel*. For fans familiar with Hercule Poirot, *The Clocks* or *Third Girl* might be worthwhile reads.

In the 1960s, Christie continued to dwell on the changes taking place in society, and she generally viewed any and all changes as bad. Phrases like "reduced responsibility" and "unfortunate childhood" appear again and again in her texts. Christie focused more of her time on trying to write plays, which she was not as successful at, as opposed to her highly popular detective novels.

The 1970s was Christie's final decade of life and productivity. She wrote nearly up until her death in 1976, although her output was greatly reduced. Only six detective novels of Christie's were published during this decade, and she had written the 1975 *Curtain* and 1976 *Sleeping Murder* during the 1940s. In *Curtain*, the famous Hercule Poirot dies.

Christie's Infamous Detectives

Christie's various mysteries created three main, enduring sets of characters—Hercule Poirot, Miss Marple, and Tommy and Tuppence. Hercule Poirot is the traditional yet eccentric detective; Miss Marple is the nontraditional, average woman who sleuths; and Tommy and Tuppence are adventurers, not detectives. Readers, however, enjoyed returning to these characters time and again.

Hercule Poirot

Hercule Poirot is a Belgian private detective with a distinctive mustache. He is what was referred to at the time as a **sleuth**. Poirot's backstory is that of a retired police detective from the Belgian police force. He is extremely eccentric, both physically and in his habits. He is short, no more than 5 feet 5 inches (1.65 meters) tall, with an egg-shaped head and a mustache. Poirot also fractures the English language with incorrect translations of French expressions. His language becomes more and more eccentric as the number of mysteries he appears in grows.

Hercule Poirot was inspired by Belgian refugees Christie encountered during World War I when she searched for a detective for her very first novel. In his first story, *The Mysterious Affair at Styles*, the "Poirot reveals all" tradition was born. At the end of each tale, Poirot details his investigation and deductions, often to a room full of people, and apprehends the culprit. As a character, Poirot was an extremely successful detective, but he was not modest, declaring himself the greatest detective in the world in *The Mystery of the Blue Train*. Christie's body of work featured Poirot often. He appears in fifty-four of Christie's short stories and thirty-three novels, including two novels that are often described as Christie's most successful: *Murder on the Orient Express* and *Death on the Nile*.

Poirot's popularity was almost frustrating to Christie. As she continued to write novels featuring his detective work, she lamented that she made him too old and mature in the very first novel. In the 1940s, she tired of the character. She wrote of his death in *Curtain: Poirot's Last Case*, but readers still enjoyed Poirot for decades because the novel remained locked in

Agatha Christie, Spy?

In 1941, Agatha Christie's novel *N or M?* was published in both the United Kingdom and the United States. The novel features a mature Tommy and Tuppence shortly after the outbreak of World War II. The title is taken from a mysterious message a British agent leaves at his deathbed, "N or M. Song Susie." The plot centers on Tommy's investigation as he goes to search for N and M, who are German spies.

Surprisingly, the name of one of the characters in the book, Major Bletchley, sparked the British intelligence agency MI5 (Military Intelligence, Section 5) to investigate Christie. The agency believed that she had somehow learned of Bletchley Park, a secret code-breaking facility. This may seem too coincidental for a government agency to launch an investigation, but Christie also happened to be close friends with Dilly Knox, who was one of the top code breakers at the secret center.

Concerned the media would break the story if Christie was questioned, agents were first sent to interrogate Knox. Knox was then sent to question Christie himself. Christie divulged that she had once been stuck on a train in the town of the same name, and simply "took revenge by giving the name to one of my least lovable characters."

The title for *N or M?* is taken from the Latin "nomen vel nomina," meaning "name or names."

The detective character Hercule Poirot has a very distinctive style.

a safe, not to be published until 1974. When it was released, Poirot received an obituary in the *New York Times*—the only fictional character to receive this honor.

Many actors have portrayed Poirot since the theatrical debut of *Alibi* in 1928. One of the most notable is Kenneth Branagh, who is slated to portray Poirot in a new 2017 film adaptation of *Murder on the Orient Express*. For many, the character is most closely associated with British actor David Suchet, who portrayed the detective over the course of more than two decades in TV adaptations of Christie's works. The character of Poirot has also lived on through Sophie Hannah, a best-selling author. In 2014, Hannah continued the character in *The Monogram Murders*, and later in 2016 with *Closed Casket*. Christie created a figure so dynamic and interesting that eighty-seven plotlines featuring Poirot were not enough. Hannah, and Poirot fans, felt that the character had to be kept alive.

Miss Jane Marple

Jane Marple, known to her fans as Miss Marple, is a nontraditional detective, an elderly spinster who lives in the village of St. Mary Mead. She first solved a mystery in *Murder at the Vicarage*, followed by several more in the group of short stories *The*

Tuesday Club Murders, also published as *The Thirteen Problems*. Unlike Poirot, Marple does not have a history of being a detective. She is extremely methodical and clever, although she will publicly deny her cleverness and exhibit extreme humility. Marple's view of the world is that human nature is generally bad and that usually the worst is true.

Her ability to solve mysteries comes from her nuanced knowledge of village life. For Marple, the smallest clue can remind her of something else which ultimately helps solve the mystery. Marple's strength as a detective is in her unusual approach; people are not as guarded with her as they would be with a traditional investigator. She is intelligent and observant, and able to disarm witnesses and suspects with her demeanor, getting them to divulge more information than the average detective.

Originally based on Christie's step-grandmother Margaret, Marple has also been portrayed in movies, television, and even a BBC radio series in the late 1990s. While Poirot is considered to be Christie's most famous character by some, Marple definitely is his equal in popularity, or at least a close second.

Tommy and Tuppence

Tommy and Tuppence first appeared in 1922 in *The Secret Adversary*. The novel itself is less a mystery to be solved than it is an adventure for Tommy and Tuppence. The duo appears in three other novels: *N or M?* (1941), *By the Pricking of My Thumbs* (1968), and *Postern of Fate* (1973). They are also featured in *Partners in Crime*, a collection of short stories published in 1929. Unique to most characters, the relationship between Tommy and Tuppence develops in time with the novels, as does their

The Detection Club

One of the oldest crime-writing clubs, The Detection Club, was formed in the 1930s as a way for a group of British mystery writers to collaborate and help each other out. There were twenty-six founding members including Anthony Berkeley, Agatha Christie, Dorothy Sayers, Arthur Morrison, R. Austin Freeman, Ronald Knox, and more. The Detection Club functioned as a social network for the writers.

Anthony Berkeley was a crime writer and contemporary of Agatha Christie. Like Christie, Berkeley is credited with being an innovator in crime writing, and he helped set the tone for future writers. He wrote under different pseudonyms, and over fifteen years he published more than twenty works of fiction. Berkeley helped set up The Detection Club after hosting a series of dinners for exceptional crime writers, especially Sayers and Christie.

The members of the club would help each other out by reviewing the technical aspects of their individual texts. For example, one writer might read Christie's work and make sure that there were enough clues along the way to point to the murderer. The club also existed to foster collaboration, and many of the members worked together and coauthored pieces, from serial radio shows to short story collections. In 1930, the BBC hired The Detection Club to write a whodunit serial for the radio called *Behind the Screen*.

Christie was heavily involved in the organization and presided as its president from 1957 until her death in 1976. It

Dorothy L. Sayers, famous writer and fellow member of The Detection Club, in 1933

still meets today (2017), with approximately three meetings taking place every year. In 2016, two texts were published in collaboration by members of the group, something that has rarely occurred since its golden age in the 1930s.

age. Over the course of the books they have a romance, get married, and even have children.

In *The Secret Adversary*, Tommy, or more formally Thomas Beresford, is a friendly young Englishman who served in World War I and was wounded. Christie describes him as ugly, but in a pleasant way, with slicked-back red hair. Prudence Cowley, or Tuppence as she is affectionately known, worked as a hospital nurse during the war. The two are childhood friends who are struggling to find work after the war in London. Tuppence is more impulsive than Tommy and is often restless and creative. The two compliment each other well. She uses her imagination to think of solutions, and he provides practical objections. When trying to solve a problem, they constantly argue but always agree on a solution in the end.

Although Tommy and Tuppence are perhaps not as recognizable as Marple and Poirot, their stories have also been adapted as a radio series, television shows, and films.

Mary Westmacott

Beginning in the late 1920s, Agatha Christie began a series of works under the pseudonym Mary Westmacott. These novels were not detective novels and were much more serious in their content. Beginning with the first one in 1928, writing as Mary Westmacott was a way for Christie to work through her many emotions. Christie created plots and characters that were similar to her own life. The characters make decisions and ponder them in ways that helped Christie think through her own life—for example, whether she was right to consent to divorce from her first husband, or whether she had been a good mother to Rosalind even though she left her to travel the world.

She wrote her first Mary Westmacott novel, *Giant's Bread*, as a way to cope with her divorce. Collins reluctantly published it in 1930. Archie Christie was the primary inspiration for the book, and it is often described as a fictional account of their relationship. The text played with ideas of love at first sight and its power over a couple.

A later Westmacott novel, *Unfinished Portrait*, focuses on Agatha and Archie's marriage, with the character of Dermot standing in for Archie. Overall, critics did not appreciate the six Mary Westmacott novels. The strongest novel, *Absent in the Spring*, receives the most acclaim for its examination of a woman's thoughts about her marriage.

In the 1940s, someone outed Christie as Mary Westmacott. Along with examining the convention of marriage and relationships between men and women, Christie also explored a wide range of social and personal issues. She had felt free to tackle these topics with anonymity. Once her secret was revealed, she ceased writing under the pseudonym, and the last book, *The Burden*, was published in 1956.

CHRISTIE
Three Blind Mice
PERSIAN MINIATURE PAINTING
A SURVEY OF PERSIAN ART
ARTHUR U. POPE
A SURVEY OF PERSIAN ART
A SURVEY OF PERSIAN ART
LEXICON
LEXICON
SCRIPTA MINOA
OXFORD
OXFORD

five

The Agatha Christie Phenomenon

"There's also a strong element of magic to her brilliance that defies analysis. How are her books able to be, simultaneously, simple enough that twelve-year-olds can love them, yet complex enough to pose an impossible challenge to a bright adult mind?" —Sophie Hannah

Christie's writings were extremely popular in her lifetime, and they still are today. Most of her detective fiction is highly satisfying to readers, inviting them to come along with some of the most unique detectives in fiction and uncover

Opposite: Christie at her home, Winterbrook, in 1950, surrounded by books

the mystery. Over time, readers knew what to expect from a Hercule Poirot or Miss Marple mystery, and they kept coming back for more. Although she lived a fascinating life, traveled the world, and worked as an archaeologist, Agatha Christie made her impact first and foremost as a detective-novel author.

By 1945, Christie was a successful author if you measured by book sales alone. A new hardcover book sold in the United Kingdom by Agatha Christie would initially be printed in a first run of twenty-five thousand copies. Beginning in the 1930s, works were also being printed in paperback, which added to her readership. By 1950, it was estimated that Agatha Christie had sold fifty million books throughout the world. She became a phenomenon, and her book sales only continue to grow.

The Paradoxes of Success

Agatha Christie's fame is somewhat of a **paradox**. She reached peak popularity at a time when the quality of her work was beginning to be heavily critiqued. In the 1950s, when her book sales were skyrocketing, her best novels—like *Murder on the Orient Express*, according to most critics—were already twenty years old. Another puzzle of Christie's success, at least to her mind, was how much stage and film adaptations added to her appeal. She was very hesitant to allow her works to be adapted, but they exponentially increased her notoriety and brought more Christie readers into the fold.

The 1945 20th Century Fox film adaptation of *And Then There Were None* catapulted Christie even more into the pop culture universe. It was the first major cinema release of an Agatha Christie book. She called it "bad" even though it did well at the box office. Shortly thereafter, a Broadway play of

And Then There Were None debuted. Neither the movie nor the play was a notable production in terms of quality. Nonetheless, Christie's prominence rose to a new level.

A variety of mediums, from television to radio, wanted to adapt her works, but Christie remained reluctant. She gave permission for Hercule Poirot to be featured on a weekly American radio show, and Christie hated it. She refused to allow her works to be dramatized on television—which today is where most new adaptations of Agatha Christie works appear.

Christie's stories also found great success on Broadway and the West End of London. However, her own original plays, which she worked tirelessly on later in her career, did not share the same acceptance as the adaptations of novels and short stories she had already written. One of the most successful in the West End was a 1925 story "Traitor Hands," which was reworked and renamed *Witness for the Prosecution* for the stage in 1953. The play was a great success, and Christie uncharacteristically threw a party in 1954 to celebrate. The production was equally as successful on Broadway, receiving a New York Drama Critics Circle Award for best foreign play. From there, *Witness for the Prosecution* was made into a movie starting Charles Laughton, Tyrone Power, and Marlene Dietrich. It was a hit and the only film adaptation of her writing that Christie ever truly liked, or so she said. The rights to *Witness* were sold for £116,000 (about $2.83 million in 2017), which she gifted to her daughter to avoid additional taxation.

Monetary Problems

Christie always struggled to enjoy her success because of lingering money and tax difficulties. In fact, the more success—financial and otherwise—that Christie obtained, the more monetary problems seemed to follow. Continuously throughout Christie's writing career there were taxation issues regarding the sales of her books in the United States. She was owed a large amount of money from book sales and royalties in America, but much of it was impounded by US tax authorities starting in 1941. Even if she received the funds from America, they might immediately be needed to pay British taxes.

By the end of the 1948, it became a real possibility that Christie would have to file for bankruptcy. Despite the threat of bankruptcy looming over Christie for years, she continued to spend money and maintain her multiple properties. Like her father, she seemed to live like money would eventually sort itself out. All of Christie's taxation issues lingered until the 1960s. She would die with a much smaller fortune (just over £100,000, or about $750,000 in 2017) than people expected her to have.

Agatha Christie Limited

One of the ways that Christie was able to combat bankruptcy and many of her monetary problems was through the creation of a company called Agatha Christie Limited. Christie's agent and publisher, Edmund Cork, thought that Christie should be turned into a limited company, which ended up being a brilliant solution. The company was created in 1955 and then employed Christie to produce novels. From that moment on, the business held the rights to the publications and paid Christie a wage. With this solution, she received essentially the same income, but less of it was given to the government through income and royalty taxes.

In 1955, the Christie Settlement Trust was also formed. The trustees bought one hundred shares in the new company,

Agatha Christie Limited, and the solution was in place. Christie had control of the company from its inception. Then, in 1957, the Christie Copyrights Trust formed to look after the rights to most of Christie's work. Creating the copyrights trust avoided another potential taxation problem—something that had happened to the estates of other authors such as George Bernard Shaw.

The creation of Agatha Christie Limited also created a structure that was able to maintain Christie's legacy after her death. Agatha Christie Limited operates today, although its ownership structure has changed. Today, 64 percent of the company is owned by RLJ Entertainment (a distributor, licensee, and developer of entertainment content), and 36 percent is owned by Christie's surviving family. As of 2017, the company is chaired and managed by Christie's great-grandson James Prichard. It manages the literary and media rights to Agatha Christie's works just as it did when the company began. In addition, the company oversees Agatha Christie Productions, which works with production companies like BBC One to produce shows, and maintains the website agathachristie.com

Agathachristie.com

Agatha Christie could not have conceived of the internet, or that it would be a place to bring together her fans long after her death with her own website. Agathachristie.com is a unique resource and concierge for those both familiar with Agatha Christie and her work, and for those who are just being introduced to her universe. A visitor can search through her works in an interactive manner, both by character (especially the main detectives like Marple and Poirot), and by title and year.

Readers can be part of a book-of-the-month club, as well as stay up to date with the latest television adaptations of Christie's works. There is a section on news related to Agatha Christie, and even contact instructions for parties looking to license the Agatha Christie brand. Pictures, information, and monetary support come from The Christie Archive Trust, which also preserves Christie's personal archives.

Christie's Audience

Christie's detective novels appeared when the genre was still relatively young and few such novels were in print. Readers enjoyed returning to the familiar characters and methodical solving of mysteries. Her books appealed to a wide range of readers with straightforward language and plot. Literary critics have stated that during the two world wars and their aftermath, readers needed to escape reality, and Christie gave them that capability. Others have argued that the detective novels provided consistency and continuity, not escapism. Regardless of the reason for their appeal, Christie's books continued to draw readers time and time again.

As Christie's popularity grew, her reading public became interested in who Agatha Christie was as a person. Reading the detective novels was not enough to satisfy her audience. Fans wanted to read about Christie in the newspaper, obtain her autograph, and write her letters that ranged from adoring to abusive to worshipping. Of course, Christie resisted becoming any kind of celebrity. She agreed to a rare photoshoot in 1953 but repeatedly turned down requests for interviews. The more famous she became, the less she wanted any kind of public life. In 1964, Christie wrote, "I think people should be interested in *books* and not their authors!"

That audience still exists today and is hungry for more Christie. World politics have changed, and there are many more writers of detective fiction, but Agatha Christie still appeals to the masses. New authors like Sophie Hannah are building on the characters that Christie created. Agatha Christie fans are still examining the ways she crafted her mysteries and constructed her plots. While fans can read Christie's works, they can also read books and other texts about those detective novels and short stories. In 2015, Kathryn Harkup published the book *A is for Arsenic: The Poisons of Agatha Christie*, in which she examines Christie's detailed knowledge of poisons and the unique ways most of her victims are killed.

Screen Adaptations

Christie's extremely large body of work continues to endure, and new readers are being introduced to her through various mediums. Although Christie is not alive and able to write new novels, luckily for audiences today, television and film can continue to adapt and interpret her works for the screen. In her life, Christie was very reluctant to allow her works to be made into movies, and she was even more hesitant to see them adapted for television. Today, the screen (television, cinema, or even streaming on a mobile device) is the way that Agatha Christie fans can continue to appreciate her grand creations and see them reinterpreted.

If a reader of Agatha Christie wanted to view screen adaptations of her work, it would be hard to know where

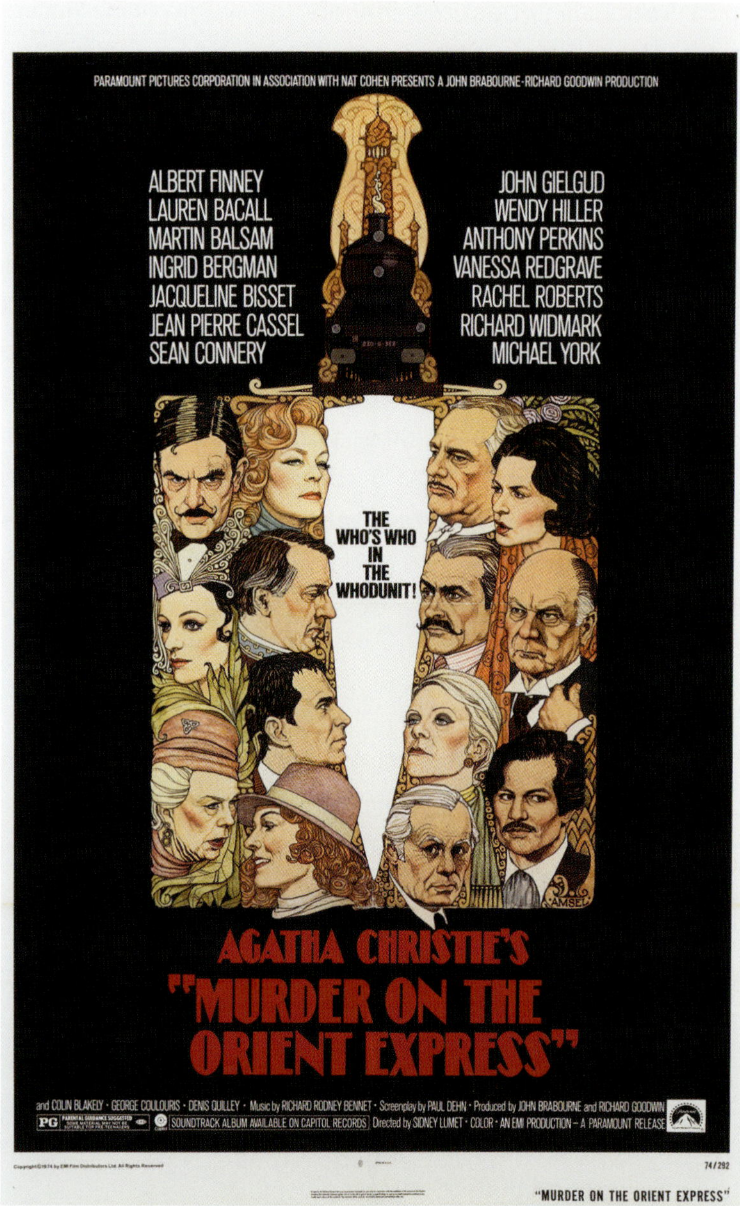

The original movie poster for *Murder on the Orient Express*

to start. Christie would likely be shocked that one internet search brings up multiple lists of critics arguing over the top five film adaptations of an Agatha Christie story. There are nearly as many on-screen versions as there are manuscripts of her work. As of 2017, Agatha Christie's IMDb (Internet Movie Database) webpage had 148 entries, and it was still growing.

One of the most successful adaptations of one of her works was the 1974 film *Murder on the Orient Express*. Christie attended its premiere—in one of her final public outings before her death—and was generally complimentary of the movie. The film stars Albert Finney as the famous detective Hercule Poirot, while the star-studded supporting cast includes Lauren Bacall, Ingrid Bergman, Sean Connery, and Vanessa Redgrave. *Murder on the Orient Express* has always been a popular Agatha Christie novel, both for the average reader and the critics. As a film it was also successful, receiving six Oscar nominations.

BBC One and Agatha Christie Productions have recently signed an agreement to produce seven different Agatha Christie works, including a new adaptation of *Murder on the Orient Express*. The new version of *Murder on the Orient Express* stars Kenneth Branagh, also the film's director, as Hercule Poirot. The extremely large cast is pulling in just as many big names as it did in 1974, this time with Johnny Depp, Josh Gad, Leslie Odom Jr., and Daisy Ridley. Bringing in actors from other cultural phenomena like *Frozen, Star Wars*, and the musical *Hamilton* will likely introduce a whole new group of people to Agatha Christie.

Inspired by Agatha Christie: Sarah Phelps

Both the detective genre and the number of authors writing crime novels have grown exponentially since Agatha Christie first began writing. Many women writers have followed in her footsteps, such as Sophie Hannah and Lindsay Jayne Ashford. Other writers, like Sarah Phelps, have worked to extend Christie's legacy by adapting her works to television movies.

In 2015, Sarah Phelps, a British television, film, and radio freelance writer, adapted Christie's *And Then There Were None* into a three-episode television miniseries. Phelps also recently finished working on adapting Christie's short story "The Witness for the Prosecution" (also published as "Traitor Hands") for television. She signed on to adapt "Witness" while she was working on *And Then There Were None*. When Phelps read "Witness" she thought it felt like a **film noir** story; it was so dark, strange, and thrilling. She was excited to adapt it. The challenge of the project was that the story itself is only twenty pages long, with very few unique details about the characters. Phelps had to decide how to visually tell the story and fill in details while also being true to the original Agatha Christie tale.

The collection *The Witness for the Prosecution and Other Stories* was recently re-released in print, with an introduction by Phelps. In it, Phelps describes the evolution of her relationship to Christie through her books. Phelps became engrossed in Christie's ability to impart contemporary color in the narrative and absorb the reader in the small details of each little mystery. While Phelps may have initially thought of Christie as merely a popular pulp author, her appreciation for Christie deepened

Actress Koo Stark in *And Then There Were None*, performed in London's West End in 1988

after examining the works and completing her own scripts. The *Witness for the Prosecution* TV adaptation aired on Boxing Day (December 26) 2016 in Great Britain.

As of December 23, 2016, Phelps has signed on to adapt a third Agatha Christie work for the screen. Phelps will be

Current State of Detective Fiction

Crime novels are still extremely popular in the United Kingdom, the United States, and around the world. Readers of detective fiction have nearly endless options. At its basic level, detective fiction centers on an investigator, either a professional or amateur, who investigates a crime—most likely a murder. By that definition, there are endless series of detective novels that readers can explore, and many identify with the novels' main detectives just as they do with Hercule Poirot.

The 1920s and 1930s are known as the golden age of detective novels. Agatha Christie, along with her contemporaries like Dorothy L. Sayers and Margery Allingham, was part of this golden age. The growth and consumption of the detective novel was like no other during this time. This period also inspired the creation of other related crime fiction. Subgenres related to crime and detective novels began to be written in the 1920s, including the private-eye, or hard-boiled, novel; the cozy crime; and the police procedural. These subgenres also gained popularity among readers who enjoyed the works of Agatha Christie.

In the 1930s, the paperback helped proliferate novels, especially detective novels, to even more people. It became more affordable for people to purchase a book. The paperback is still crucial to book sales, but today an entire series of Hercule Poirot mysteries can be purchased as digital text or audio and downloaded to a device with just one click. Films and television shows are also available to rent or purchase online. For those who prefer a physical book, paperbacks can be ordered and delivered right to a reader's doorstep. Fans of Agatha Christie can quickly be immersed in a mystery through nearly any medium they choose.

While online, Christie's audience can get further suggestions for detective fiction. Amazon.com might suggest they read a modern-day Hercule Poirot mystery, perhaps one by Sophie Hannah, or an Agatha Christie–inspired mystery, like *The Woman on the Orient Express* by Lindsay Jayne Ashford. Crime fiction appears on network television and streaming services as well.

adapting the novel *Ordeal by Innocence* for a collaboration between BBC One and Agatha Christie Productions. In fact, the collaboration is going to be bringing forth seven different Agatha Christie works for the small screen.

Agatha Christie's Autobiography: Controlling Her Legacy

While Christie was still alive, she received countless letters and offers to have her biography written. She did not want anyone to write her biography and believed that readers should be interested only in the books she wrote. Disliking the idea of someone else telling her story, Christie opted to write it herself in her aptly titled *Autobiography*. She took her time and worked away at it for fifteen years, between 1950 and 1965.

Ultimately, it was not published until after her death. Although it has been used as a source for quite a few biographies about Agatha Christie, it is not a useful resource as a factual account or for verifying when major life events took place. Christie was already sixty years old when she began writing it, and her memory imperfect. Her intent was not to provide a timeline of her life but to share her feelings and recollections.

The Theater and Her Critics

Towards the end of her writing career, Christie struggled to extend her legacy to the theater. Despite the long engagement of *The Mousetrap*, she did not have the enduring success on the stage that she wanted. The plays she composed did not have the strength of her books. Many critics and casual consumers of Christie's works have often commented that she produced a mystery better than almost anyone. While she

The West End, where Agatha's plays debuted, as it looked in 2017 with *The Mousetrap* still on the marquee

did write excellently crafted tales, her books are much more than that. The plot, the mystery, and the characters all come together in a way that keeps readers coming back, but the plays she wrote did not share the same recognition.

Christie was advised by many, including Edmund Cork, not to pursue the theater. Regardless of this advice, in 1961 she wrote three small plays. Somehow the plays always found a venue, but the performances were given scathing reviews, often stating that the playwright (Christie) was out of touch with life and society. Christie continued to try to be known as a playwright, and her reputation began to suffer. Some circles began to consider her talent diminished. Even with this tarnish on her reputation, her book sales continued to grow steadily through the 1960s. Through the very end of her career, Christie was always authentic. She pursued the writing projects she wanted to work on and never once compromised so that she

Sophie Hannah

Sophie Hannah is the unofficial heir to Agatha Christie for many fans, although the two are not related. When Hannah was twelve years old, her father gave her a copy of an Agatha Christie book, and she spent the next two to three years reading everything Christie had written. Hannah lives in Great Britain, and like Christie she is an internationally known author, but she writes psychological crime fiction as opposed to detective fiction. She also writes short stories and poetry as well as crime fiction. Her work has been published in thirty-two languages, and some of her works have even been adapted for television.

Hannah resurrected the Hercule Poirot character by writing a new mystery novel featuring him as detective. She was granted permission from Matthew Prichard, Christie's grandson, who was the chairman of Agatha Christie Limited at the time. Hannah pursued the project. She met with Christie's family and told them her idea for a plot, submitted an outline, and eventually she was given the authorization to use the character. Subsequently, she became the authorial heir to Agatha Christie, and she created a new novel. In 2014, *The Monogram Murders* was published, featuring Poirot as a character.

Reviewers both loved and grumbled over Hannah's reincarnation of Poirot. Readers appreciated it enough that there was a market for a second new Poirot mystery. In 2016, Hannah's next Poirot novel, *The Closed Casket*, was published. Both *The Monogram Murders and The Closed Casket* are set in a time well before Poirot's death and are not a retelling of a Christie Poirot mystery.

Hannah enjoyed the challenge of writing an Agatha Christie character. In order to make the novels authentic, she had to make sure not to just copy Christie's writing style but to meld Christie's Poirot with Hannah's own authorial voice. To do this, Hannah created a new first-person narrator to tell the story for *The Monogram Murders*. Beyond that, she reread thirty-three of Christie's Poirot mysteries and focused on the character himself. Hannah told the *New York Times*, "For me, writing this book is my way of writing a love letter to Agatha Christie and Poirot ... Agatha's the best-selling author that ever lived. I don't have any power to effect Agatha's legacy at all."

could sell more books. Even when Collins wanted an edit, a different cover for a novel, or a slight revision, Christie would stand up for her original idea, almost to a fault.

Christie's Place in the World

In addition to the large and popular body of work Christie left behind, her creations have been adapted numerous times for television and cinema, resulting in an enduring success that cannot be understated. In remarks about her after her death, multiple examples were given to demonstrate her pervasiveness in world culture. Behind William Shakespeare, Agatha Christie is considered the most widely read author in the English language. Even more remarkable, her detective novels have been translated into more foreign languages than any other books, with the Bible being the only exception. If someone stacked all US editions of Christie's *Peril at End House*, they would extend from Peoria, Illinois, to the moon. The sheer volume of production is staggering when thinking only about the physical books, but Christie's body of work, and the subsequent creations she inspired, extends way beyond the paper texts. In 2017, Christie's legacy ranges beyond libraries and bookstores to e-readers and the internet. Fans can find Agatha Christie on DVDs, PBS, the BBC, and streaming online.

With this staggering contribution to literature and media, it might be easy to forget Christie was more than a prolific author with a voluminous output of novels, short stories, and plays. She also lived an extremely interesting life. While Christie did not think her personal life or thoughts made her any more valuable as an author, her fans, critics, and historians all find both her works and her experiences fascinating. The entire

Christie attends the premiere of *Murder on the Orient Express* in 1974.

time she was writing detective novels, she traveled around the world, lived through two world wars, worked as a dispenser and an archaeologist, and devoted time to her marriages and her family. She overcame great disappointments and moments of grief, and took charge of her life. Even when married, she pursued all her endeavors as an independent woman. She was also a woman who found time for leisure and enjoying the people and places she loved. Christie would be astonished to discover she has become a legend, known as one of the most successful and prolific writers of all time.

Glossary

apothecary An older word for pharmacist, someone who dispenses prescriptions and medications.

aria A long, accompanied song for a solo voice in an opera.

autodidact A person who is self-taught, most often without any formal education.

deportment The behavior, manners, or demeanor of a person.

Dictaphone A small recorder used to record speech for transcription.

diplomatic Relating to international relations, or the practice of negotiations between nations.

film noir French for "black film" or "dark film," refers to a category of film characterized by pessimism and fatalism.

genre Category or subject matter, determined by similarities in form or style.

gentry People of good social position, specifically in the United Kingdom.

governess A woman employed to teach children in a private household.

industrialize To build up a system of industries and factories in a country or region.

matriarchy A social or familial organization in which descent and relationship are reckoned through the female line.

paradox A thing, person, or statement that involves contradictory elements.

pseudonym A fictitious name, usually used by an author.

psychology The study of behavior and the mind.

radio play An acoustic show broadcast on the radio. During the height of the form's popularity in the 1940s, actors' performances were often enhanced with sound effects and music to help listeners visualize the story.

reticent Not revealing one's thoughts or feelings easily.

serial Regular installments of a story or play on television, radio, or in a periodical.

sleuth A detective, or person who investigates.

telegram A message sent with a telegraph, which used electronic signals to transmit long-distance on a wire, and then delivered in printed form.

Chronology

1890 Agatha Mary Clarissa Miller is born on September 15.

1901 Her father, Frederick Miller, passes away.

1912 Meets Archibald Christie for the first time.

1914 Marries Archibald Christie. World War I begins. Joins the Voluntary Aid Detachment.

1917 Qualifies as an apothecaries' assistant.

1918 World War I officially ends on November 11.

1919 Rosalind Margaret Christie is born.

1920 Her first book, *The Mysterious Affair at Styles,* is published.

1922 *The Secret Adversary*, Christie's second novel, features the characters Tommy and Tuppence.

1926 Christie's mother, Clara Miller, dies. Christie mysteriously disappears for eleven days.

1928 Agatha and Archibald Christie divorce. Christie travels to Baghdad for the first time. She rides on the Orient Express.

1930 Marries Max Edgar Lucien Mallowan. *The Murder at the Vicarage*, Christie's first Miss Marple mystery, is published.

1939 World War II begins.

1941 MI5, British Military Intelligence, investigates Christie.

1943 Matthew Prichard, Christie's grandson, is born.

1945 World War II ends.

1952 *The Mousetrap* opens on November 25. It eventually becomes the world's longest continuously running play.

1955 Christie receives the first ever Grand Master Award from the Mystery Writers of America. Agatha Christie Limited is formed.

1956 Is appointed Commander of the Order of the British Empire (CBE).

1958 Becomes president of The Detection Club.

1961 Exeter University in the United Kingdom awards her an honorary doctorate.

1970 Matthew Prichard becomes director of Agatha Christie Limited. He would later become chairman in 1976.

1971 Christie is promoted Dame Commander of the Order of the British Empire (DBE).

1974 The film *Murder on the Orient Express* premieres.

1975 The last of Christie's Poirot novels, *Curtain: Poirot's Last Case*, is published. In this book, Poirot dies.

1976 Christie passes away on January 12 after several years of poor health.

2014 Sophie Hannah publishes *The Monogram Murders* and revives the character of Hercule Poirot by placing the timeline of the novel before Poirot's death.

2015 Christie's great-grandson, James Prichard, becomes chair of Agatha Christie Limited.

2016 *Closed Casket*, Sophie Hannah's second Poirot novel, is published.

Further Information

Books

Edwards, Martin. *The Golden Age of Murder: The Mystery of the Writers Who Invented the Modern Detective Story*. New York: HarperCollins, 2015.

Green, Julius. *Curtain Up: Agatha Christie: A Life in the Theatre*. New York: HarperCollins, 2015.

Harkup, Kathryn. *A is for Arsenic: The Poisons of Agatha Christie*. New York: Bloomsbury Publishing, 2015.

Websites

Agatha Christie

http://www.agathachristie.com

Explore the entire Christie universe, including a look at the newest TV adaptation of Agatha Christie's story "Witness for the Prosecution."

Agatha Christie Birthday Celebrations

http://www.agathachristiefestival.com

The International Agatha Christie Festival hosts a birthday celebration for Christie each year in Torquay. This site offers details about the festivities and guests as well as information on Christie.

Agatha Christie's Riviera

http://www.englishriviera.co.uk/agathachristie/home

A travel website dedicated to exploring Agatha Christie's life through her hometown and region.

Films

And Then There Were None

http://www.imdb.com/title/tt3581932/?ref_=nv_sr_1

Learn about Sarah Phelps's television adaptation of Christie's novel into a three-episode miniseries.

Murder on the Orient Express

http://www.imdb.com/title/tt0071877/?ref_=nv_sr_2

Find out more about the Oscar-winning 1974 movie adaptation of one of Agatha Christie's best-loved novels.

Bibliography

Acocella, Joan. "Queen of Crime: How Agatha Christie Created the Modern Murder Mystery." *New Yorker*, August 16, 2010. http://www.newyorker.com/magazine/2010/08/16/queen-of-crime.

Allsop, Laura. "Agatha Christie's Secret Life as an Archaeologist." CNN, March 12, 2011. http://www.cnn.com/2011/WORLD/europe/03/12/uk.christie.writer.archaeology.

Alter, Alexandra. "Sophie Hannah Talks About Rebooting Agatha Christie's Poirot." *New York Times*, September 9, 2014. http://artsbeat.blogs.nytimes.com/2014/09/09/sophie-hannah-talks-about-rebooting-agatha-christies-poirot.

Cawthorne, Nigel. *A Brief Guide to Agatha Christie.* Philadelphia: Running Press Book Publishers, 2013.

"Changes in Divorce: The 20th Century." Parliament.uk. Accessed January 5, 2017. http://www.parliament.uk/about/living-heritage/transformingsociety/private-lives/relationships/overview/changesindivorce.

Christie, Agatha. *An Autobiography*. New York: HarperCollins, 1977.

Doyle, Martin. "Agatha Christie: Genius or Hack? Crime Writers Pass Judgment and Pick Favourites." *Irish Times*, September 16, 2015. http://www.irishtimes.com/culture/books/agatha-christie-genius-or-hack-crime-writers-pass-judgment-and-pick-favourites-1.2351699.

Gill, Gillian. *Agatha Christie: The Woman and Her Mysteries.* London, UK: Pavilion Books, 2016. https://books.google.com/books/about/Agatha_Christie.html?id=0RKuDQAAQBAJ.

Hannah, Sophie. "No One Should Condescend to Agatha Christie—She's a Genius." *Guardian*, May 16, 2015. https://www.theguardian.com/books/2015/may/16/guardian-book-club-sophie-hannah-agatha-christie-death-on-the-nile.

King, Stephen. "Stephen King: Can a Novelist Be Too Productive?" *New York Times*, August, 27, 2015. https://nyti.ms/2kppVjp.

Lask, Thomas. "Hercule Poirot Is Dead; Famed Belgian Detective." *New York Times*, August 6, 1975. http://www.nytimes.com/1975/08/06/archives/hercule-poirot-is-dead-famed-belgian-detective-hercule-poirot-the.html?_r=0.

Mason, Emma. "The Golden Age of Murder: Agatha Christie and the Detection Club." *History Extra*, June 11, 2015. http://www.historyextra.com/article/culture/golden-age-murder-agatha-christie-and-detection-club.

Morgan, Janet. *Agatha Christie A Biography*. New York: Alfred A. Knopf, 1984.

Thompson, Laura. *An English Mystery: Agatha Christie*. London, UK: Headline Publishing Group, 2007.

Zemboy, James. *The Detective Novels of Agatha Christie: A Reader's Guide*. Jefferson, NC: McFarland and Company Publishers, 2008.

Index

Page numbers in **boldface** are illustrations. Entries in **boldface** are glossary terms.

And Then There Were None, 79, 96–97, 104, **105**

apothecary, 16

aria, 38

Ashfield, 20–21, **20**, 28, **29**, 30–31, **30**, 33–35, 44–45, 50, 52, 55, 66, 77

Ashford, Lindsay Jayne, 104, 107

autodidact, 35

BBC, 89–90, 99, 103, 108, 112

Berkeley, Anthony, 90

Bletchley Park, 86

Bodley Head, The, 75–78

Branagh, Kenneth, 88, 103

British Empire Exhibition Tour, 53–54, 78

cars, 23, 54, 68–69, **68**

Chagar Bazar, 63–64

children's literature, 42–43, **42**

Christie, Agatha

adaptations, 6, 67, 69, 88–89, 92, 96–97, 99–101, **102**, 103–105, **105**, 107–108

archaeology, 6–7, 19, 54, 60, 63–65, 96, 113

critical reception, 78, 80, 82–84, 93, 96, 100, 108

daughter, 52, 57, 60, 65–67, 76, 83, 92, 97

Detection Club and, 90–91

detective fiction, 5–6, 15–16, 19, 22–23, 25, 31, 54, 57, 64–65, 67, 72–86, **75**, **87**, 88–89, 92, 95–97

disappearance, 56–57, **59**

early life, 6–9, **10**, 11, 20, 23, 25, **26**, 27–36, **29**, **37**, 38, **39**, 40–43, 72

early writing, 38, 40, 72

legacy, 7, 88, 99–101, 103–105, 107, 110–113

marriages and suitors, 6, 11–13, 15, 18–19, 41, 44–47, **48**, 49–58, 60–61, **61**, 63–67, 69, 75, 78–79, 92–93, 113

Mary Westmacott novels, 57, 65, 80, 92–93

music, 36, 38, 40, 46

nonfiction, 30, 38, 64, 108

relationship with mother, 6, 9, **10**, 21, 25, 32–33, 52, 55

theater, 5, 69, 81, 84, 96–97, **105**, 108–109, **109**

travel, 6–7, 9, 11, 19, 33–36, **37**, 41, 52–54, 59–61, 63–65, 69, 73, 77–78, 80, 96, 113

wartime work, 15–16, 18, 35, 51, 72, 113

Christie, Archibald, 12, **12**, 15–16, 18, 30, 41, 44–47, **48**, 50–59, 63, 65, 72, 75–78, 93

Come, Tell Me How You Live, 64

coming-out party, 9–11, 41

Cork, Edmund, 64, 78, 98, 109

Curtain, 84–85, 88

deportment, 36

depression, 52, 55, 67

Detection Club, The, 90–91

detective fiction

conventions of, 23, 106

early development of, 22–23

growing popularity of, 6, 22–23, 25, 100, 106

subgenres, 106

today, 101, 106–107

Dictaphone, 74

diplomatic, 13

divorce, 24, 56–59, 62, 78–79, 92–93

Doyle, Arthur Conan, 23

film noir, 104

genre, 23, 100, 104, 106

gentry, 33

governess, 9

Great Depression, 14–15

Greenway, 66, 69

Hannah, Sophie, 88, 101, 104, 107, 110–111

industrialize, 7

Iraq, 19, 59–60, 63–64

Mallowan, Max, 19, 60–61, **61**, 63–67, 69, 79

Man in the Brown Suit, The, 54, 69, 77–78

Marple, Miss Jane, 23, 84, 88–89, 92, 96, 100

matriarchy, 32, 42

Miller, Clarrisa, 6, 8–9, **10**, 15, 21, 25, 27, 30–35, 38, 40–41, 44–45, 47, 50–56, 61, 66, 77

Miller, Frederick, 8–9, 27–29, **29**, 31–35, 98

Miller, Margaret, 8–9, 27, 34–36, 38, 40, 43, 53, 72

Model T, 68–69, **68**

Mousetrap, The, 5, 69, 81, **81**, 108, **109**

Murder of Roger Ackroyd, The, 78–79

Murder on the Orient Express, 69, 73, 85, 88, 96, **102**, 103, **113**

Mysterious Affair at Styles, The, 6, 72–77, 75, 85

nature versus nurture, 83

N or M?, 86, **87**, 89

opera, 36, 38, 40, 46, 49

paperback books, 96, 106–107

paradox, 96

Phelps, Sarah, 104–105, 108

Poe, Edgar Allan, 22–23

Poirot, Hercule, 23, **75**, 76–77, 79–81, 84–85, 88–89, **88**, 92, 96–97, 100, 103, 106–107, 110–111

Potter, Beatrix, **42**, 43

pseudonym, 40, 57, 80, 90, 92–93

psychology, 79, 110

radio play, 81

reticent, 28

Sayers, Dorothy L., 11, 90, **91**, 106

Secret Adversary, The, 54, 74, 77, 89, 92

serial, 54, 67, 76, 90

servants, 9, 23, 28, 30–31, 32, 80, 82–83

sleuth, 84–85

stereotypes, 80

Suchet, David, 88

Syria, 63–64

telegram, 60

Tommy and Tuppence, 15, 74, 84, 86, 89, 92

Voluntary Aid Detachment (VAD), 15–16, **17**, 51

Wagner, Richard, 38, 46, **46**, 69

West End, 40, 81, 97, **105**, **109**

Winterbrook, 66, **94**

Witness for the Prosecution, 97, 104–105

women's suffrage, 24

Woolley, Leonard and Katherine, 60, 63

World War I, 6, 12–16, 18–19, 22–24, 51–52, 55, 62, 72, 75–77, 85, 92

World War II, 13, 15, 18–19, 22–23, 25, 66–67, 86

About the Author

Meghan Engsberg Cunningham received her BA in English and American studies from St. Norbert College and her MA at the University of Wisconsin–Milwaukee. She completed her master's-degree thesis on Charles Chesnutt's novel *The Marrow of Tradition* along with the texts that were precursors to the Harlem Renaissance. Meghan has spent time working with student writing as a writing center tutor at St. Norbert College and then as an assistant coordinator at the UW–Milwaukee Writing Center. She currently works in financial litigation. Meghan lives in Milwaukee with her husband, Stephen, and son, Liam. Together they enjoy reading, running, and traveling. Her other titles include *Bill "Bojangles" Robinson, W. E. B Du Bois, and Jesse Jackson.*